'Mike Bell is well known for setting up
Network, and for explaining succinctly and clearly
in education according to summaries of rigorous research. Your
students will benefit from these highly effective methods.'

Geoff Petty, *author of 'Evidence Based Teaching'*

'We do not want evidence – we want good evidence, evidence that
we can interpret to make a difference in the school and class, and
we want big picture thinking based on these interpretations of this
evidence. Mike Bell does all this by using Visible Learning and four
other sources to give us confidence that when we apply evidence
in the classroom, learning will improve.'

John Hattie, *author of 'Visible Learning'*

'I was delighted to see that the book does not just focus on what's
worked in research studies, but gives practical advice on what
might be less effective and where stopping or cutting back might
leave some space for more effective methods. The book provides
a summary of research-based practices from different sources,
including our Teaching and Learning Toolkit, then also provides an
explanation from cognitive science about learning which helps to
explain *why* these practices might be effective, so helping to explain
the underlying rationale.'

Steve Higgins, *Education Endowment Foundation*

'Mike has run several sessions for us. We have asked him back
because teachers found his presentation of the evidence convinc-
ing, the methods suggested practical and the brain-based explanations helpful.'

Marie-Dominique Reza, *Vice principal, DLD College, London*

'Mike ran a session with our teaching team, focusing on effective
teaching methods, arranged as five steps. Our staff found it very
practical and easy to follow. They were immediately able to apply
the learning, and we are continuing to implement the methods.'

Janet Robinson, *Director of Performance,*
Borders College, Galashiels

The Fundamentals of Teaching

Teachers are bombarded with advice about how to teach. *The Fundamentals of Teaching* cuts through the confusion by synthesising the key findings from education research and neuroscience to give an authoritative guide. It reveals how learning happens, which methods work best and how to improve any students' learning.

Using a tried-and-tested, Five-Step model for applying the methods effectively in the classroom, Mike Bell shows how you can improve learning and eliminate time-consuming, low-effect practices that increase stress and workload. He includes case studies from teachers working across different subjects and age groups which model practical strategies for:

1. Prior Knowledge
2. Presenting new material
3. Setting challenging tasks
4. Feedback and improvement
5. Repetition and consolidation.

This powerful resource is highly recommended for all teachers, school leaders and trainee teachers who want to benefit from the most effective methods in their classrooms.

Mike Bell taught science in a state secondary school and then ran the Evidence-Based Teachers Network (EBTN). He has run successful training courses on evidence-based methods in dozens of UK schools and Further Education (FE) colleges.

The Fundamentals of Teaching

A Five-Step Model to Put the Research Evidence into Practice

Mike Bell

Routledge
Taylor & Francis Group

LONDON AND NEW YORK

First published 2021
by Routledge
2 Park Square, Milton Park, Abingdon, Oxon OX14 4RN

and by Routledge
52 Vanderbilt Avenue, New York, NY 10017

Routledge is an imprint of the Taylor & Francis Group, an informa business

British Library Cataloguing-in-Publication Data
A catalogue record for this book is available from the British Library

Library of Congress Cataloging-in-Publication Data
Names: Bell, Mike, author.
Title: The fundamentals of teaching : A 5 step model to put the research evidence into practice / Mike Bell.
Description: New York : Routledge, [2021] | Includes bibliographical references and index.
Identifiers: LCCN 2020018495 | ISBN 9780367358648 (hardback) | ISBN 9780367358655 (paperback) | ISBN 9780429342318 (ebook)
Subjects: LCSH: Teaching. | Teacher effectiveness.
Classification: LCC LB1025.3 .B448 2021 | DDC 371.102--dc23
LC record available at https://lccn.loc.gov/2020018495

ISBN: 978-0-367-35864-8 (hbk)
ISBN: 978-0-367-35865-5 (pbk)
ISBN: 978-0-429-34231-8 (ebk)

Typeset in Arial
by SPi Global, India

Contents

Foreword

I can see this book becoming a firm favourite for a great many teachers given the scope of ideas and research covered and the intelligent, down-to-earth blend of theory and practice through the case studies. As well as putting so many ideas in one place, this book also pulls off the clever trick of feeling timeless and contemporary all at once. It's going to last!

I don't think there has ever been a better time to be a teacher. At long last, the worlds of education research and frontline teaching practice are talking to each other in a dynamic fashion and I sense a sea change in teachers' and leaders' attitudes to the idea of developing an evidence-informed profession. Increasingly, over the last five years or so, the level of teacher engagement with the insights from cognitive science and other research fields has grown significantly. There's an enormous appetite for knowledge about how students learn and, with limited time to invest, what the best bets might be for the classroom activities and strategies that we design and enact.

At all times, however, it's not simply a case of teachers taking ideas from research and implementing them in some kind of mechanistic, standard fashion. Far from it. The challenge is to make sense of research evidence in the context of teaching your subject to your particular students who arrive with a wide variety of prior knowledge, attitudes to learning and life experiences. It's complex. But, importantly it's not so complicated that we can't do it well and do it better. Schools wouldn't work at all if students didn't have a great deal in common in the way they learn or if it were not the case that some strategies simply are more effective than others.

In Graham Nuthall's seminal *Hidden Lives of Learners* he expressed deep reservations about teachers being forced to follow recipes; of teachers being told what to do. He suggests that *'teaching is about sensitivity and adaptation. It is about adjusting to the here-and-now circumstances of particular students'*. However, he also goes on to add this important qualification: *'As a teacher, you make adaptations. You must. The important question is: what adaptations do you make? You can do it by a kind of blind trial and error, but it would be much better if you knew what kinds of adaptations were needed, and why.'*

That final 'why' is vital. 'Evidence-informed wisdom' is the goal; a blend of teachers' experience and expertise informed by evaluating their own practice and the successes and difficulties their own students experience, together with insights from research underpinned by a model for learning that explains why things work and don't work.

This is where a book like *The Fundamentals of Teaching* comes in. In essence, Mike Bell's excellent book is a guide to developing the evidence-informed wisdom teachers need. He has done a superb job of synthesising ideas from multiple sources to great a clear coherent framework for exploring and delivering effective teaching. There's an important examination of the evidence and the science of how learning works, reinforcing a shared understanding of concepts and terminology. Mike's Five-Step learning cycle builds on a wide range of studies to provide a simple model from which teachers can springboard in different directions, according to their contexts.

The great strength of the book then comes from the extensive exploration of putting the evidence into practice, modelling the learning process through the way readers are encouraged to engage with the book. As we encounter a range of strategies to deliver each of the steps, we are invited to consider: What do we know already? What's the underlying model and evidence base? What new learning do we need to move forward? Can we make sense of it via some case study examples? Now, how well have we understood the concepts and their applications? This repeated structure is clever and powerful. It makes you stop to think about your own knowledge all the way through and, in doing so, succeeds in building a model for teaching far greater than the sum of its parts.

In his concluding comments, Mike suggests that we 'arm ourselves with the evidence' as we embark on our continued journeys through the profession, bombarded by commentators on all sides. I'd say that he's given us plenty of ammunition.

Tom Sherrington

Acknowledgements

The starting points of my journey to writing this book were conversations with Michael Shayer and Denise Ginsburg about their work on Cognitive Acceleration. They gave me insights into the learning process from the learner's perspective and introduced me to abstract and concrete thinking.

The main influence on this book has been Geoff Petty. His book *Evidence-Based Teaching* was my first introduction to the fact that 1000s of experiments had been done in education and that these had been assessed for effectiveness. His book showed how the dry statistics, such as those by John Hattie, could be translated into practical classroom tasks; a tradition I hope I have developed here. Geoff also gave me initial opportunities to run training sessions for staff at schools and colleges which are the foundation for this book. The idea of the Learning Cycle is a development of one he used.

The material in the book, including the Five Steps, emerged from the process of discussion with other members of the Evidence-Based Teachers Network and feedback from training sessions in numerous schools and FE colleges over several years.

I am grateful to Helen Payne for talking to me about the process of writing a book in ways which implied that I would succeed.

In developing the drafts I have received tremendous help from David Ruddle who has given me detailed feedback from a teacher's perspective on the whole text. My daughter, Veronica Bell, did a similarly valuable job from the perspective of someone unfamiliar with the material.

I am grateful to Annamarie Kino at Routledge for advice, support and encouragement during the process of building the book. Britto Fleming Joe at SPi Global for his care with the layout, Caro Hogan for help choosing the cover and my daughter Katey Bell.

The book has a number of case studies for each method in Section 2. These are all derived from real teacher experience (including that of the author). Examples were gathered from dozens of teachers to give real-life examples of the methods in action. I would like to thank all those who contributed. All contributions are anonymised, so do not name individuals here.

Finally, I am grateful for my mild dyslexia which has been beneficial while compiling this book. I struggle with long texts and so have been naturally drawn to research reviews, rather than original papers. I tend to see connections and similarities, rather than differences; see the big picture, rather than focussing on detail and understand things best through diagrams.

Mike Bell
Cambridge, UK
2020

Introduction

We all want to improve the learning of our students, but what should we try? As teachers we are bombarded with books, websites, government policy, gurus, fads and enthusiastic colleagues. How can we choose what to spend our time doing?

This book aims to answer that question by bringing together a wide range of research and presenting it in ways which can be easily applied in your classroom.

Thousands of experiments have been done in classrooms and psychology. Several teams of researchers have combined the results of many of these experiments to create lists of effective methods or principles of effective teaching.

The book uses five of these 'research reviews' and then groups the most effective methods into a five-step learning process. It also uses knowledge about the brain and learning to provide explanations for the effectiveness of these methods.

We live at a significant time for teaching. Perhaps for the first time we have enough evidence to say with some confidence that we know what is likely to work (and what is unlikely). That is why this book is called *The Fundamentals of Teaching*. It is neither the opinion of the author nor the results of individual experience; it is the consensus from a whole range of evidence.

The methods covered are not age- or subject-dependent. The research shows that, with very few exceptions, people of all ages and in all subjects learn roughly in the same way and all benefit from the effective methods. (One exception is that long homework does not seem to help in primary school, but is effective by age 12.)

Throughout the text 'learners' are referred to as 'students' as this term applies to learners of all ages. People who are training to be teachers are referred to as 'trainees' or 'trainee teachers'.

WHO IS THIS BOOK FOR?

Nearly all teachers will find this book useful:

- Trainee teachers – looking for a basic introduction to 'what works and why'.
- Ambitious teachers – who want to get even better results.
- Successful teachers – who are curious to understand why their results are so much better than those of their colleagues.
- Senior teachers – who want to know the best ways to improve the skills of their staff.
- Exhausted teachers – who want to get the same results with a bit less work and stress.
- Manipulated teachers – who want to check that their managers' demands have some evidence to back them.
- Demoralised teachers – who struggle to improve their results, however hard they work.

HOW TO USE THIS BOOK

Section 1: Evidence provides the evidence that shows which methods are effective and gives an explanation for the learning process which shows why these methods work so well. Although you can use Section 2 without this explanation, Section 1 gives you a mental model of the learning process which will help you diagnose problems in your classroom and choose effective remedies. It professionalises your role, giving you control of which methods to apply rather than simply picking a method from a list.

Use this section to improve your understanding of the learning process.

Section 2: Effective classroom practice takes you through five stages of the learning process. Each stage has several effective methods. The chapter explains a method, gives an explanation for how it works, offers a range of anecdotes from teachers who have used the method and, finally, an exercise for you to use to practice it.

Using the insights you have into the learning process, this section enables you to choose and apply the most appropriate methods for your class.

Don't try and change too much at once. If you are already getting average or above-average results you are already a fantastic teacher. Focus on one or two methods and practice with them for at least six months. (For more guidance, see under 'Staff development' in Section 3.)

Having chosen the method you plan to experiment with, try to read at least one other source from the 'Further reading' before trying the method. There are usually about three of them – all chosen because they explain how to use the method (rather than a theoretical discussion).

Section 3: Using resources effectively looks at some of the evidence which needs to be applied outside the classroom, often on a whole-school/-college practice. It includes effective staff training, use of teaching assistance, best use of technology and policies to reduce workload.

Use this section to audit the way you currently use resources and make any changes needed to improve cost-effectiveness.

DEVELOPING ANY SKILL

The evidence shows that the most important people in a school or college are the teachers and that developing the skills of the teacher is the best way to improve results. Before looking specifically at teaching skills, let's see how we develop any skill.

This diagram shows the evidence of how we improve our performance with any skill. Let's look first at the skill of playing the guitar.

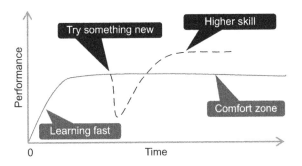

Your early learning is represented by the continuous grey line. When you start (at time 0), your performance is very low; as you practice, however, you learn fast and your performance increases. Initially, you just want to play one tune and need chords in C major. You practice for a while and eventually get to the comfort zone where you are confident to play the tune for your family or friends. If you do nothing else, you should be able to continue at this level of skill for years.

However, if you want to play other tunes, with chords in different keys, you will have to follow the dashed, darker line when you try something new. Initially, when you try the new chords, your performance drops dramatically, so you would probably practice in your room with the door closed, or perhaps only during your guitar lesson. However, after some time you develop an even higher level of skill and can play more tunes for friends and family.

Now let's look at someone developing teaching skills. Most of us start at a low level of performance and, if a lesson goes badly, you reflect, talk to your mentor, etc. and try and improve, so, you are learning fast.

However, with practice, the lesson goes well; the student's behaviour was OK and they seem to have learned something. You are no longer sweating! Many of us get into this comfort zone and just carry on teaching that way; as a result, our skills can get stuck at that level. Some claim that teachers, on average, reach their maximum effectiveness after only about five years.

The question we need to ask is: 'Why don't we teachers practice with new methods and continuously increase our skills?'

SAFETY WHEN PRACTICING

Part of the answer is that 'up-skilling' is harder in teaching than it is in guitar-playing. If you're trying something new on your guitar, you would just do it quietly in your bedroom. You could turn the volume down if it was an electric guitar, and nobody would know how bad you were until you were confident enough to go and play in front of somebody again. The problem in teaching is that your learning happens in front of a class.

Consequently, when 'up-skilling' your teacher's skills, only try one or two new things at a time. Keep practising those until you are skilled. If you're training in tennis, you wouldn't try and 'up-skill' every part of your game at the same time. When you try out a new teaching method, you need to be prepared for the fact that it may not go well for the first three times, and doesn't start to get better until about five times. You're not reasonably skilled until 10 times, and it doesn't become part of your everyday practice until you've done it about 25 times.

To deal with the likelihood that the lesson may go badly – perhaps because you are unfamiliar with the method, or you made resources which did not work first time – try it only for a short time initially: maybe 5 minutes in the lesson, or perhaps do it at the end. Be prepared for the fact that you're going to feel that the lesson went worse, and therefore push through until the third repeat, just as you would if you were practising the guitar. There's no point in trying something once and thinking 'No, that didn't work', because practically everything doesn't work first time – which perhaps explains why so many teachers stick in their comfort zone.

DO I NEED TO USE ALL THESE METHODS?

No. The evidence shows that it is not so much the individual methods which make the difference, it's whether you are taking your students through the Learning Cycle. If you are checking and repairing their prior knowledge, linking to it in your presentation, effectively communicating the new material, teaching in accessible chunks, setting tasks which challenge the students, providing feedback and requiring an improvement, giving spaced repetition and assessing learning with a high pass rate, you are doing what the evidence shows. The individual methods simply give opportunities for this to happen.

HOW *NOT* TO USE THIS BOOK

Even though the methods have been shown to be effective, it is important that individuals, managers or politicians do not turn them into a 'must do' checklist. Teachers can lose their autonomy and become judged, not by the quality of the learning in their classroom, but by whether they are doing the things on the checklist.

For instance, when deciding whether to use Collaborative Methods, the decision should be based on a learning need, not simply because it is 'on the list'. If working in groups contributes to the Learning Cycle for your students and subject, then go for it.

Do not use this book to increase the work/stress of the teacher. If you adopt a new practice, make sure you give up something less effective to make time.

If you are already a highly effective teacher, you probably have a good grasp of the learning process (even if it is intuitive rather than conscious). Deepen your understanding of the learning process and do not change your practice too much at once.

PROMOTING SUCCESSFUL LEARNING

The evidence is very optimistic. It shows that almost every teacher can improve the learning of their students if they start using some of these methods. It also shows that almost all students can learn if they are taken through the main steps of the Learning Cycle.

Use Section 1 to develop your understanding of the evidence and the learning process.

Use Section 2 to apply your skill and judgement to choose the methods you will try in your classroom.

Use Section 3 to identify any changes needed in whole-school/college policy to ensure that human and money resources are used effectively.

WHAT THIS BOOK DOES NOT COVER

This book covers effective classroom methods and an understanding of the learning process. It does not cover other areas of a teacher's work such as behaviour management, being a form tutor or organising a parents' evening.

1 EVIDENCE

This section looks at evidence: identifying reliable evidence, where we can find it, what the evidence shows and what neuroscience can tell us about the learning process.

This section identifies the most effective methods which have good evidence behind them. These methods are then explained in more detail in Section 2.

This section is in three chapters.

Chapter 1: ***Getting reliable evidence.*** Not all evidence is the same quality. The need for a measurement to compare effectiveness. How evidence empowers the teacher.

Chapter 2: ***Sources of evidence.*** Five major compilations of educational evidence are compared and combined into Five-Steps; arranged in the order in which you would use them in teaching a topic.

Chapter 3: ***Brain-based explanation.*** Insights from Educational Neuroscience are used to provide explanations for the effective methods identified in Chapter 2.

1

Getting reliable evidence

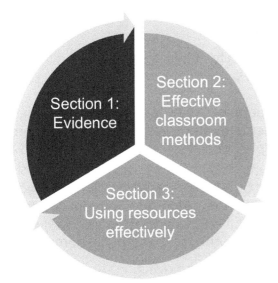

Ch1: Getting reliable evidence

Ch2: Sources of evidence

Ch3: Brain-based explanation

To improve the learning of our students, we need to know which teaching methods work best. This chapter explains:

- How to identify reliable evidence.
- What measure we can use to compare the effectiveness of different methods.
- The five main sources of evidence used in this book.
- The combined list of effective methods from those five sources.

WHAT IS RELIABLE EVIDENCE?

Getting reliable evidence is not easy. Even if we read the original research ourselves we encounter problems. People who study evidence (to decide what is reliable), point out that, for non-research experts, it can be confusing to read individual research papers because:

- We all have 'confirmation bias': we tend to pick out evidence which supports our own preconceptions.
- Individual research papers can sometimes be contradictory: we need to combine results from different sources.
- It is difficult to work out the quality of the research.

Quality of evidence

Not all evidence is the same quality. Let's look at two different studies:

- Study 1 is carried out on 24 students in one class by one researcher who creates their own assessment after 3 weeks. The results are compared with the students' previous results.
- Study 2 involved 250 students in 10 classes across 5 schools where the lessons are taught by trained classroom teachers and the progress assessed 2 years later using independent assessments such as GCSE results. The results are compared with several 'control groups': other classes which are taught the same topic in their usual way.

In Study 1, you cannot be sure if the effect they measure is simply created by the enthusiasm of the researcher, for instance. By testing the method in different classrooms we can iron out these individual effects. The use of control groups allows us to compare similar classes, taught the same course in the same year.

This is similar to the way medicine uses 'randomised control trials' (RCTs) for new treatments. Here patients are assigned to one of two groups:

- A 'control group' who are given a dummy (placebo) pill or the existing treatment.
- The 'experimental group' who received the new treatment.

Participants do not know which group they are in so the researchers can be more confident that any effect they see is due to the new treatment.

USING RESEARCH REVIEWS

To make our choices we need reliable evidence. By 'reliable' we mean that, if other people test the method, they are likely to come to a similar conclusion about its effectiveness. This means we cannot rely on individual pieces of research, but need to combine the results from several different experiments. This book makes use of the work of several teams of researchers have sifted through a wide range of evidence as a 'research review' (which compares the results of several individual studies) or 'meta-studies' (which combines the numerical evidence about how effective the method is).

This means that the reviews we use here are both more reliable than individual research papers and has also been tested on different subjects and student ages.

The use of research reviews is very common, for example, doctors rarely read original research (unless it is about their speciality) and rely on research reviews produced by expert groups like NICE or the Cochrane UK.

The importance of measurement

One problem we face is that, according to the evidence, nearly everything which has been tested which aims to improve learning, seems to be effective! This means that the most important question for teachers is not *'Does it work?'*, but *'How well does it work compared to all the other things I might try?'*

It makes sense for you to invest effort only in things which will make a big difference. As we will see in Section 3 'Using resources effectively', it takes a lot of time and effort to develop your skill with a new method to the point where it becomes a natural part of your lesson planning.

A common measure

In many areas of life we use a common measure. For example, if apples are sold by the kilo, we can compare one shop's prices with another. However, if they were sold by the bowlful, we could not as different shops may have different size bowls.

'Effect-size' is a commonly used measure used in research to compare the results of different experiments on the same scale. The diagram illustrates how it is calculated. It compares the 'control group' (who were taught in their usual way) with the 'experimental group' (who are taught with the method you are testing).

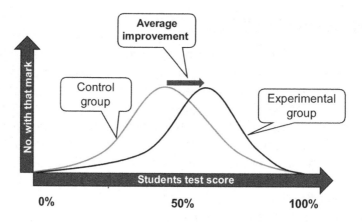

FIGURE 1.1

Along the bottom, we have the score students get in their test at the end of the topic. Up the side are the number of students who got that score. In a typical class, a few get low scores, a few high scores and many get scores nearer the average.

If the experimental method is effective we see a shift in the graph. Some still get low scores (ability or effort) and those with high scores can only improve a bit. However, the average moves. If we divide the average improvement by a measure of the spread of the scores (standard deviation) we get a figure called 'effect-size'.

This is a great way to compare results because it doesn't matter what maximum mark for the test was.

As a rule of thumb, the effect-size (ES) means:

- 0: no effect
- 0.2: small effect
- 0.4: average effect
- 0.6: good effect
- 0.8 and above: high effect.

Without this type of measurement, teachers can easily be misled by enthusiastic researchers, managers, politicians, etc. They regularly tell teachers to use *their* approach because 'the research shows it is effective'. Always be wary of any claims like this; ask for the effect-size and, if the policy requires a lot of work to implement and the ES is low, pause.

If you are required to implement a low-effect method, one strategy is to smile, agree, but not to implement it! If challenged, refer back to the objective (raising standards, better behaviour, etc.) and say you *have* implemented it – but using a more effective, evidence-based strategy. If you feel confident of a positive reception, you could suggest the evidence-based strategy as an alternative.

Mistaking what is visible for what is effective

Without some numbers to tell us how effective a method is, it is easy to fall into the trap of using methods which sound good, seem sensible, but lack evidence to support them.

The graph below is constructed from one of the research reviews which compares the effectiveness of 140 different methods.

The scale along the bottom shows the effect-size and the scale upwards shows the number of methods having that effect.

You will see that, according to the evidence, nearly everything has a positive effect! The average effect is 0.4. This suggests that we shouldn't try anything below 0.4 (unless it involved almost no work or expense).

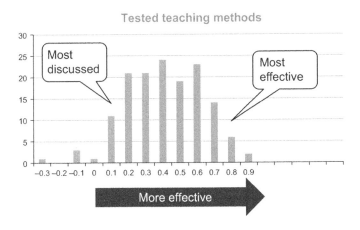

FIGURE 1.2

The most effective methods are on the right, but if we identify the methods which politicians, journalists and parents favour, we find them mostly on the left, low-effect side.

One explanation for this is that non-experts are always looking for something visible that they can see: smart uniform, visible marking of students' work, academy status, etc. The most effective methods are often invisible to the non-expert. Learning is not itself visible and needs to be assessed, so non-teachers may not notice your use of graphics, your improved questioning technique or the care you have taken to space out your students' practice.

EMPOWERING THE TEACHER

Some teachers are concerned that using evidence could become '*one more stick with which to beat teachers*'. However, this is not the case in other professions. The 'sticks to beat teachers' have mostly been about compulsion to use specific methods, for example:

- Particular interpretation of the evidence on 'assessment for learning'.
- Insistence that phonics is 'the answer' for all pupils.

Most other professions are liberated by evidence. Doctors or engineers do not feel oppressed by their anatomy or structures textbooks. A good knowledge of the evidence empowers the individual teacher and gives them autonomy and the opportunity to say 'no' when asked to carry out a counter-evidence task.

FURTHER READING

Churches et al. (2017) *Neuroscience for Teachers*. Preface. Meta-analyses and effect sizes.

Geoff Petty (2018) *Teach Even Better*. Ch 14 Sifting educational evidence.

2

Sources of evidence

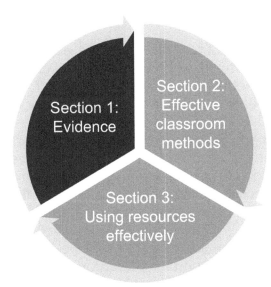

Ch 1: Getting reliable evidence

Ch 2: Sources of evidence

Ch 3: Brain-based explanation

Fortunately for us 1000s of experiments have been carried out world-wide, both in classroom and laboratories, all of them aimed at finding out what works best in learning. Of course, it isn't possible for an individual teacher to digest it all, so we are fortunate that several teams have sifted the evidence for us and generated their own lists of effective methods.

This book also make use of the new understandings of the 'brain and learning' to provide explanations for the effective methods.

The three main sources are:

- Classroom evidence (where the methods are tried by teachers with regular students).
- Educational Psychology (where experiments are often started in laboratories).
- Educational Neuroscience (which explains what is happening in the brain).

It is possible to find fault with any of these sources:

- When comparing classroom experiments it is sometimes difficult to be sure that two methods are the same, even if they have the same name.
- Psychology experiments are often started in laboratories and so we may not be able to translate the results into the classroom.
- Most scientists agree that we are very far from being able to say '*The neuroscience shows..., therefore, in your classroom you should...*'. We may never get there without the usual extensive trials.

But, what if we stop relying on one source and apply the evidence only if it is backed up by another? What if we only implement a classroom method if it can be explained by neuroscience? What if we don't implement psychology research unless it has had classroom trials?

At first this may sound far-fetched. '*Surely it'll take decades to do all that extra research?*' I hear you say. The good news is – we don't have to wait; there already exists enough cross-referencing for us to explain the learning process, suggest effective ways to improve it, understand why some students struggle (in different ways) and have ways to help them.

In this book combines five of these major 'research reviews' to create the Five-Step Learning Cycle. We then cross-reference it to the neuroscience to check that an explanation is available. Only then do the methods 'make it' to the book.

CHOOSING THE REVIEWS

The five main sources, the brain-based explanations and the diagrams in this book have been used and tested in teacher-training sessions over eight years. They have been honed by the feedback from teachers at sessions organised by the Evidence-Based Teachers Network (EBTN).

The five research reviews used here are all from well-known and respected teams who have brought together a significant number of individual research reports and combined their results to create their lists of effective methods or principles of effective teaching.

The first three sources are from classroom experiments – the method is tried out on whole classes and the results compared with the control-group classes. The other two are from Educational Psychology.

Classroom evidence

Three major research reviews are used here. They do not generate lists which are exactly the same, (largely due to different methods and purposes), but, as we will see, they have more in common than at first appears.

- *Classroom Instruction that Works*. Marzano/Dean
- *Toolkit*. Education Endowment Foundation (EEF)
- *Visible Learning for Teachers*. John Hattie.

We show that, by combining the most effective methods from the three lists, we can give a clearer approach to implementing the evidence.

Dean: Classroom Instruction that Works. Ceri Dean et al. 2012

First published in 2001 by a team under Robert Marzano, this list is from the 2nd edition, 2012, edited by Ceri Dean. The Marzano and Dean team looked only at classroom methods, so we have used their whole list here. The team combined a smaller number of high-quality studies.

(The book is divided into nine chapters. However, some chapters include more than one method, so they are separated in our list.)

Methods:

1. Setting objectives
2. Providing feedback
3. Reinforcing effort
4. Cooperative learning
5. Cues and questions
6. Advance Organisers
7. Non-linguistic representations
8. Summarising
9. Note-taking
10. Homework and practice
11. Similarities and differences
12. Generating and testing hypotheses.

EEF: Toolkit. 2019

The Education Endowment Foundation (EEF) is an independent charity dedicated to breaking the link between family income and educational achievement.

They do this by:

- Summarising the best available evidence in plain language for busy, time-poor teachers and senior leaders, and providing practical tools to make use of this evidence.
- Generating new evidence of 'what works' to improve teaching and learning.

The EEF originally generated their list to advise teachers on how best to help disadvantaged students. This does not affect its usefulness, as almost all the effective methods work whatever the subject, age or ability of the student. EEF also set the highest standards for quality of evidence. The list is being regularly updated; we have used the list available in 2019.

Their list of effective interventions also contains things which are not classroom methods like small-group tuition, peer tutoring and one-to-one teaching. These can guide the way we support struggling students and appear in Section 3 – *Using resources effectively.*

Method:

1. Feedback
2. Metacognition and self-regulation
3. Reading comprehension strategies
4. Homework (secondary)
5. Mastery learning
6. Collaborative learning
7. Early years interventions
8. One-to-one tuition
9. Oral language interventions
10. Peer tutoring
11. Phonics
12. Outdoor adventure learning
13. Small-group tuition
14. Digital technology
15. Behaviour interventions.

Hattie: Visible Learning for Teachers, 2012

The team under John Hattie, initially based at Auckland University, New Zealand, scoured the world for education research, converted all the results onto the Effect-size scale and then crunched the numbers to see the average result. First published in 2009 as *Visible Learning*, we have used a more recent list from the 2012 book *Visible Learning for Teachers.*

Hattie's team included everything connected with student achievement, including influences on the student, the curriculum and the teacher. We have selected only those methods which can be applied in any classroom.

1.   Feedback
2.   Reciprocal teaching
3.   Spaced v massed practice
4.   Metacognitive strategies
5.   Classroom behavioural
6.   Vocabulary programmes
7.   Student prior achievement
8.   Self-verbalisation/self-questioning
9.   Problem-solving teaching
10. Not labelling students
11. Comprehension programmes
12. Concept mapping
13. Co-operative v individualistic
14. Direct instruction
15. Mastery learning
16. Worked examples
17. Peer tutoring
18. Phonics
19. Outdoor adventure programmes
20. Interactive video
21. Goals
22. Questioning.

Comparison of the lists

At first sight, it looks as if the three lists are significantly different. This partly reflects the way they were created, but we do see similarities. For example:

■   Feedback and co-operative learning appear high on all three lists.
■   Phonics and metacognition both appear on two lists.
■   Sometimes, when we read the more detailed descriptions, similar methods have different titles, e.g., *Generating and testing hypotheses* and *Problem-solving teaching*

The next section looks at two sources of evidence from Educational Psychology.

Educational Psychology evidence

We used two research reviews which summarise the evidence from cognitive psychology research:

- *Principles of Instruction*. Barak Rosenshine. International Academy of Education (IAE)
- *Organizing Instruction and Study to Improve Student Learning.* Institute for Educational Sciences (IES).

IAE: Principles of Instruction

The International Academy of Education (IAE) is a not-for-profit scientific association that promotes educational research, and its dissemination and implementation.

Written by Prof. Barak Rosenshine, this booklet combines evidence from three sources: cognitive science, the classroom practices of master teachers and tested methods to support students learning complex tasks.

They extracted ten principles:

1. Daily review of previous learning
2. Present new material using small steps
3. Ask questions
4. Provide models
5. Guide student practice
6. Check for understanding
7. Obtain a high success rate
8. Scaffold for difficult tasks
9. Independent practice
10. Weekly and monthly reviews.

IES: Organizing Instruction and Study to Improve Student Learning

Prepared for the US Department of Education, this practice guide was written by seven professors at US universities. It is is modelled on practice guides in the health services.

They extracted seven recommendations:

1. Space learning over time
2. Interweave worked example solutions and problem-solving exercises
3. Combine graphics with verbal descriptions
4. Connect and integrate abstract and concrete representations of concepts

5. Use quizzing to promote learning
6. Help students allocate study time efficiently
7. Help students build explanations by asking and answering deep questions.

COMBINING THE EVIDENCE

At first glance, these five sources of evidence do not look similar! To see the similarities and find the methods with the most evidence, in the table below the methods are arranged in the order you might use them to teach a topic.

Main section	Method	EEF	Dean	Hattie	IAE	IES
Orientate to learning	Behaviour	✓		✓		
Step 1: Prior Knowledge	Assess Prior Knowledge		✓	✓	✓	✓
	Fill missing knowledge	✓		✓		
Step 2: Present new material	Working Memory limit				✓	
	Link to Prior Knowledge		✓	✓		
	Advance Organisers		✓			
	Multi-sensory approach		✓	✓		✓
	Link abstract to concrete					✓
Step 3: Set a challenging task	Graphical Organisers		✓			
	Modelled/worked examples			✓	✓	✓
	Metacognition	✓		✓		
	Collaborative methods	✓	✓	✓		
	Thinking tasks		✓	✓		✓
Step 4: Feedback for improvement	Feedback (self, peer and teacher)	✓	✓	✓		
	Questioning			✓	✓	
Step 5: Repeat	Spaced repetition			✓		✓
	Deliberate practice	✓	✓		✓	
Step 1a: Re-assess	Mastery learning (high 'pass' level)			✓	✓	

Explanation of the steps

Orientation to learning

Things which should be in place before the topic lessons start and provide the environment for learning.

Step 1: Prior Knowledge

Used prior to starting the topic – seeing what the student already knows and filling in gaps.

Step 2: Presenting new material

Methods and important considerations to use when presenting new material to your students.

Step 3: Challenge

Ways to set your students tasks which are most likely to make their learning of the new material effective.

Step 4: Feedback

Methods to show the student how to improve. Note the importance that they implement the feedback, not simply receive it!

Step 5: Repetition

Methods which give the student the opportunity to develop long-term memories by revisiting the new material over time.

Step 1 (repeated): Re-assessment

This is Step 1 of the next part of your topic. You need to be sure that the level of understanding is high before moving on.

The Learning Cycle

This diagram illustrates the circular nature of the Five Steps.

FIGURE 2.1

How well do the five sources agree?

Although they have been generated by different teams for different purposes there is a great deal of overlap between the lists as shown by the number of ticks in the table for a particular method.

Interestingly, the only method which comes from Educational Psychology which is not already on the combined list from the classroom experiments is 'Working Memory limit'. As we will see in the next section, Educational Neuroscience explains why ignoring this limit significantly reduces the potential learning of your students.

You will note that not every method on the five lists is present here. This is because:

■ Sometimes the same method is given a different name by different authors.

■ Sometimes an individual method is an example of a more general method.

■ We are looking for common ground.

■ We want something which is simple to apply.

In the next chapter we take a look at what neuroscience tells us about the learning process. This new understanding gives us brain-based explanations for why the effective methods, identified by classroom and psychology experiments, work.

Additional sources of evidence

What you will see is that, despite their differences, these five sources have a high level of agreement and together give us a clear picture of the learning process.

Indeed, there is now a high level of agreement among all educationalists who focus on evidence. The disputes in education are largely disagreements between well-argued opinions, not evidence.

Consequently, there are several other sources which are based on evidence which all fit with the Five Steps we use here. We will be referring to them when they provide good illustrations for the chapter. It is possible to plot each of these sources against the Five-Step table and show they are compatible.

■ Petty (2018) *Teach Even Better.* Oxford University Press.

■ Wiliam (2011) *Embedded Formative Assessment.* Solution Tree.

■ Sherrington and Caviglioli (2020) *Teaching WalkThrus.* John Catt.

- Allison and Tharby (2015) *Making Every Lesson Count.* Crown House.
- Deans for Impact (2015) *The Science of Learning.* Deans for Impact.
- Churches et al. (2017) *Neuroscience for Teachers.* Crown House
- Chartered College of Teaching (2020) Impact No. 8: *Cognition and learning.*
- Fletcher-Wood et al. (2018). *The Learning Curriculum.* Institute for Teaching.
- Coalition for Psychology in Schools and Education (2015). *Top 20 Principles from Psychology for PreK–12 Teaching and Learning.*
- Brown et al. (2014). *Make It Stick.*

There is an emerging consensus among those educationalists who look at the evidence. For example, the 'Six Principles' in Allison and Tharby: *Making Every Lesson Count* are:

1. Challenge
2. Explanation
3. Modelling
4. Practice
5. Feedback
6. Questioning.

All six appear in the Five Steps used here.

TOWARDS A 'THEORY OF LEARNING'

When we first start looking at evidence of effective methods, we need to focus on the quality of the evidence for that method. However, when we see the big picture which the evidence paints, we start to see that it is not so much a list of effective methods, but more an overall understanding (or theory) of the learning process.

An analogy

A group of archaeologists are interested in a site. They have found some artefacts, done some geo-physics and read the archives, but they do not agree on what the site was used for. Some think it is a Roman villa, others that it is a medieval castle. As the dig starts, new artefacts and walls emerge and the researchers find new sources of written evidence. At a certain point the archaeologists come together and assess all the evidence they have. In quite short time they all agree that the evidence points to a big picture of the site: it is not a Roman villa, it is a medieval castle.

This book suggests we have reached that point in education. Among those who look at the evidence, there is now a high level of agreement.

The need for an explanation

So far we can say that these five sources point to a big picture. What is missing, however, is an explanation of why these methods are effective (and why other methods and policies are less effective). Without an explanation, these are just checklists of methods which leave the teacher vulnerable to being instructed to use them or not knowing which to choose in their specific context.

Once we know 'why', we will not only know which methods to use in our classroom, but also be able to explain our choice to others: we will have become professionals.

We can get that explanation by looking at the brain. In the next section we see what brain studies relating to learning – Educational Neuroscience – has to tell us.

FURTHER READING

Ceri Dean. (2012) *Classroom Instruction That Works*. ASCD.
Education Endowment Foundation. *Toolkit*. Online resource.
John Hattie (2012) *Visible Learning for Teachers*. Routledge.
Institute for Educational Sciences. (2007) *Organizing Instruction and Study to Improve Student Learning*.
Barak Rosenshine. (2012) *Principles of Instruction*. International Academy of Education.

3

Brain-based explanation

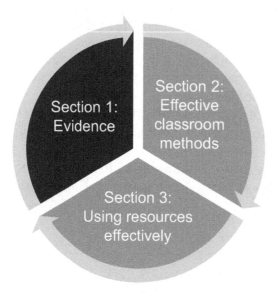

Ch1: Getting reliable evidence

Ch2: Sources of evidence

Ch3: Brain-based explanation

This section provides a brain-based explanation of the learning process which explains the effectiveness of methods identified by the evidence. It is not used to provide classroom guidance.

Some people are rightly concerned about the misuse of neuroscience in education. They warn us that we are very far from being able to say 'The neuroscience says… So we should …'. Indeed, without classroom experiments, we will never be able to make such statements. (There is nothing special here – this is true for all science. Unless we 'test the hypothesis' we cannot progress our understanding.)

However, learning happens in the brain, so this should not deter us from seeing whether this new understanding of the brain can help us explain:

- How learning happens.
- Why some people struggle to learn.
- How we can help all students learn more easily.

HOW MUCH DO WE NEED TO KNOW? IT ALL SOUNDS COMPLICATED

We do not go into any detailed neuroscience here. If you are interested we list some more detailed books at the end of this chapter. A basic understanding of how the brain forms long-term memories etc. provides the explanations we need to understand the methods in Section 2 work so well. Luckily, we need neither much detail nor complex terminology to do that.

PLASTICITY

Plasticity is the ability of the brain to change with practice. This is one of the most optimistic ideas in education. It says that the current ability of your student is not fixed; learning changes the brain. (The word 'plastic' here is used to mean 'able to be moulded' as in Plasticine, not as in 'plastic bag'.)

When we look at our own body, we see that nearly every part of the body has a specific function. Hands hold things but do not talk. Stomachs digest food but do not pump blood.

However, when we look at the brain, things are not that clear. One way to see this is to look at what happens when someone has a stroke.

Strokes happen when the blood supply to a part of the brain is cut off. That part dies and does not recover. The job that part was doing is lost. The stroke victim may lose the use of an arm, or their speech or some other function. All the other functions may well continue to be as good as before.

However, many stroke patients start to recover their lost function almost immediately and, with good therapy, can sometimes almost completely recover. This can happen because of this characteristic of 'plasticity' – the ability of the brain to re-wire itself. A different part of the brain takes over the lost function.

Although our students do not have strokes, many appear to have weak functions – things they seem unable to do. Some have difficulty in reading or spelling, others say they cannot pay attention, others that they are 'no good at maths', etc. While these statements are true at the time, *plasticity* shows that they do not need to be permanent.

This is good news both for the struggling student and also for the teachers trying to help. Change is possible. As we will see in this chapter, the process of change is the same as for learning. If we take a student through the Learning Cycle, then permanent changes are made to their brain. The student no longer has the same brain.

Looking back at Hattie's list of effective methods, we see that *'Not labelling students'* is a method with a high effect-size! This is amazing news: it means we can get better results simply by stopping using terms like 'dyslexic' or even 'gifted and talented'.

This does not mean that labels are entirely useless. If they are used to explain that there is a weakness that needs to be addressed and the explanation leads to the student actually engaging with the extra help, then the label can be useful. It is when it is used as an excuse or reason to maintain the weak skill that it becomes unhelpful.

FORMING LONG-TERM MEMORIES

When repetition leads to long-term memories, there are physical changes in the brain.

What are memories in the brain?

It's important to understand the significant differences between memories in the brain and memories on a computer/phone etc. Table 3.1 highlights some of them.

Table 3.1

Computer memories	Brain memories
Are formed instantly when you hit 'save'.	Will disappear very quickly unless they are repeated.
Are recalled exactly as they were recorded.	Are rarely accurate.
Do not change by being 'remembered'.	Change over time as they are remembered and used.
Take up a lot of memory space – the hard drive gets full.	Take up little space and seemingly the brain has near-infinite capacity.
Only speed limits the amount that can be remembered at one time.	Clear limits to what can be learned at one time.

The explanations for these differences become clear once we see what memories are in the brain.

Basic brain unit – the neuron or nerve cell

Our brains are made up of billions of nerve cells or neurons, all connected together. We form memories when some of these pathways become strengthened by being repeatedly used. This is a simplified diagram of one cell.

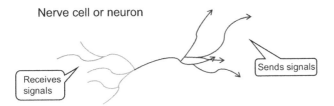

FIGURE 3.1

One end receives signals from other cells and the other transmits them. In reality, cells have far more connections than shown here, a baby's brain cells each have around 500 connections.

Cells linked at synapses

The cells are not directly connected. The signal runs along the cell as an electric impulse, but between each of the cells there is a tiny gap – a synapse. To get across the gap we have chemical messengers – neurotransmitters – which trigger the signal in the next cell. If the synapses in a particular pathway are stimulated repeatedly, they undergo a chemical change which means this pathway is permanently open. This is called 'long-term potentiation', and is how long-term memories are formed.

However, if the pathway is used only once (for instance, the student only encounters a new idea in one lesson) the pathway remains open for a while, but, within a day or so, it reverts back to its original state and is ready to be re-used.

Analogy

Imagine a grass field with a gate on either side. No-one has walked in the field for a while, so every route across the field is possible. The first person starts to make a path with the route they take. If someone else follows soon afterwards, they can follow the track and their journey also strengthens the track. If however no-one passes for a few days, the grass grows back and no track is visible.

If, however, people regularly walk that path it will become permanent: everyone who wants to cross the field and leave by the gate will follow the same route.

The field is like our brain. The gates are the connection we need to remember something. The repeated use is our repetition. The lost pathway is our forgetting if we do not revisit the material.

What's happening in the brain?

This diagram shows a synapse close-up. The incoming signal travels along the left-hand cell and triggers neurotransmitters into the gap in the synapse. These then bind to the small and large gates on the receiving synapse. The small gate opens and allows some small chemicals to flood in which stimulate the signal in the receiving synapse. (The gap is tiny, so this happens very quickly.) However, the large gate does not open because, like every other synapse which is not part of a long-term memory, it is blocked and can only be unblocked from the inside.

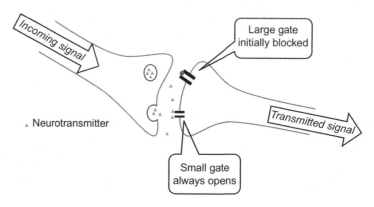

FIGURE 3.2

Let's say your student only thinks about the new learning during one lesson. The small gate stays open and they seem to have 'learnt it'. However, by the next day, the small gate has closed and there is no long-term memory.

Another student does their homework that night, or mulls it over on the bus, or answers a question from a friend, or sees something which reminds them of the new learning. This happens several times. The small gate is repeatedly stimulated and lots of chemicals flood in. Then something remarkable happens: the chemicals push the blockage out of the large gate. The large gate is now permanently usable. Next time this student thinks about this topic, both the small gate and the large gate open. This makes it much more likely the signal will be transmitted as the large gate also allows larger chemicals to flood in.

Then further changes take place in the synapse. More gates develop in the synapses of this pathway so that, in future, this pathway is even stronger. This 'long-term potentiation' is a permanent physical change. The student has a long-term memory.

This means that some sort of re-visiting of the material is vital to create long-term memory. Some students give us the impression that they learn something instantly because they are the ones who do remember the new learning the following week. However, a closer look shows that they have done the repeats themselves, either by mulling it over, or by discussion with friends or because they already knew most of the material and the lesson simply provided the 'Aha!' moment where it all made sense.

We have all experienced the frustration of this in our classroom. We teach our students something and they seem to understand. They even do the task we set them. But a few days later they seem to have completely forgotten what they learned. Some even claim they did not have that lesson! Once we know how memories are formed in the brain, this is not surprising. All the synapses on the new pathways we worked so hard to activate have now reverted to zero. It's not that they have forgotten – it's that they never formed long-term memories.

(This also means that any idea of judging learning or progress in one lesson is a myth. You can only be sure they have long-term memory if they can recall the information a week or month later.)

Spaced repetition

Figure 3.3 shows one way to imagine the learning process. When we first learn something, our recall can initially be near 100%. However, over the next few hours, the recall starts to fade. Our memory follows the grey, dashed 'forgetting' curve on the graph.

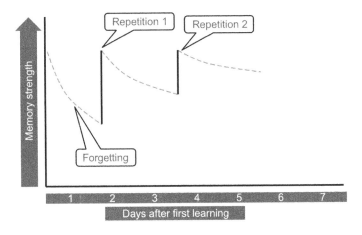

FIGURE 3.3

If there is no repetition, the first 'forgetting' line will continue down until the memory strength is zero. However, repeating the same pathway (shown by the black 'Repetition' lines) gradually slows the forgetting process so that, after several repetitions, we have good long-term memory.

Memories as links

So we have seen that memories are links between brain cells and that these links can be made permanent by repetition, but how can a 'memory' just be 'links'?

Let's look at what happens when a baby creates a memory of their first cup, which is green.

When they first are given the cup, they do not recognise it nor know what it is for. However, once they start to drink a whole series of connections start to form: visual shapes, colours, physical feelings and emotional responses.

At the most basic level our brains are wired to detect shapes and colours. If someone takes ten pictures of the green cup on their digital camera, the camera has to store the green colour for each of the pictures. The brain, by contrast, simply links to the green part of the colour detection area. Every green object is linked there – so saving a huge amount of space.

The same is true of nearly all the other aspects of the cup, as illustrated in Figure 3.4.

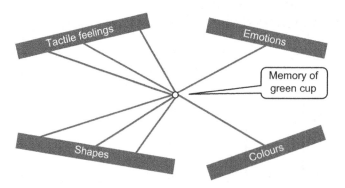

FIGURE 3.4

The great insight from the neuroscience is that what we call the 'memory of the cup' does not contain the information about the cup in the way the memory on a computer would. In the brain the memory is simply the links to the component parts.

Linking memories

The brain saves even more space by linking new experiences to ones already stored as memories.

In this example, we create the concept 'kitchen furniture' simply by linking together things which we already know are found in a kitchen such as 'table' and 'chair'. From this it is fairly obvious that we cannot understand or retain the concept 'kitchen furniture' unless we already have memories of things you would find in a kitchen.

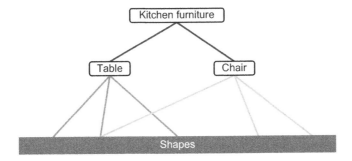

FIGURE 3.5

In the next example, you may be trying to teach your students about the Pope. You may do so by linking this new idea to ones you think most of your students already know, like 'king', 'church' and 'man'. Earlier in their life (or in your lessons) your students would have learned about what a 'king' is by linking it to their ideas about 'father', 'crown' and 'country'.

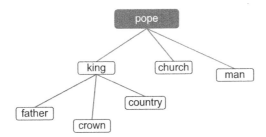

FIGURE 3.6

You may have used language such as 'You know how the king is the head of the country? Well, the Pope is the head of the church'.

The importance of prior knowledge is expanded further in Section 2. Later we also see that the Marzano/Dean team identified '*similes and analogies*' as great ways to link new knowledge to what the student already knows. Here we can see why they work so well.

WORKING MEMORY

Working Memory is not the same as long-term memory and has limited capacity.

Working Memory is the space we use to 'think about' something. When we say something like 'I was conscious that she was looking at me' or 'I love this music', what we really mean is that our Working Memory was filled with this at that moment.

Working Memory capacity

There is some debate about how many items the Working Memory can hold, but some simple tests can show us how much useful capacity it has. Science has shown there are at least two types of Working Memory:

- An Auditory Loop, which is where we are repeating words to ourselves (sometimes called 'Phonological Loop').
- A Visual-Spatial Sketchpad, which holds visual and spatial information.

Auditory Loop capacity

If you were to be shown a card with three random numbers on it for a few seconds – say 361 – and you were then asked to recall the numbers 10 seconds later, almost everyone could succeed at this task. However, as we increase the number of digits – 73914 then 987014532 – we would get to a point where we simply could not recall them. This capacity is different for different people, but is usually in the range of 5–9 digits.

Visual-Spatial capacity

One way to test this is to give the student a set of 3 × 3 grids which are blank, similar to the ones on the left-hand side of this diagram.

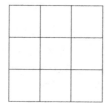 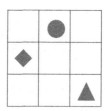

FIGURE 3.7

Then, you tell the students that shapes, circle, triangle or diamond, will appear (using cards or slides) in some squares for a few seconds (as in the right-hand section of the diagram). After a few seconds, they need to mark their blank grid with what they saw.

Initially, only one shape appears in one square and almost all your students manage the task easily. However, as you increase the number of shapes, students start to make mistakes. The number of shapes/positions where they start to make serious, regular errors is their visual-spatial Working Memory capacity.

Age and Working Memory

Working Memory gradually increases in childhood, which helps explain why younger pupils struggle with complex ideas which they find easier a few years later. Here is a diagrammatic version of the pattern.

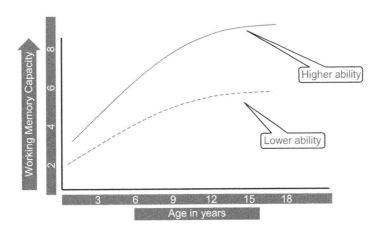

FIGURE 3.8

Consequences of limited Working Memory

Experiments show that Working Memory capacity is key to successful learning. Students with low capacity learn more slowly than those with more capacity. There is also some evidence that harder, more abstract ideas require more Working Memory and hence are much less accessible to low Working Memory students. There is a close link between Working Memory capacity and IQ test results.

This means that it is easy to overwhelm your students by presenting too much new material at once. In Section 2 we return to the question of Working Memory limit with specific examples of how to make sure you don't overload your students' Working Memory. It is one of the important factors in the Learning Cycle.

LINKING LONG-TERM AND WORKING MEMORY

If Working Memory has such a small effective capacity (5–9 items), how do we manage to think about anything? Even something like planning a meal has many more than nine items.

The answer is that, if some of the material is held in long-term memory, it takes much less space in Working Memory. This network of links is sometimes referred to as a 'schema'.

```
                    pope
                   /  |  \
                  /   |   \
             king  church  man
            / |  \
           /  |   \
      father |   country
           crown
```

FIGURE 3.9

If we look back to the example of teaching your students about the Pope, if they do not know about it, the idea must take four spaces in Working Memory: pope, king, church and man.

Working Memory use if the concept is not known						
1	2	3	4	5	6	7
The Pope,	a man	who is like	the king	of the church,	went	to Rome.

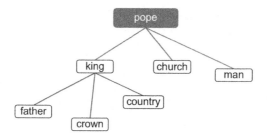

FIGURE 3.10

However, once the concept 'Pope' is stored in long-term memory, it only takes one space and we can start to teach these students new material about the Pope.

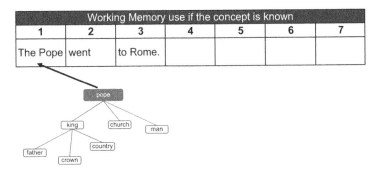

FIGURE 3.11

This helps explain why methods, which requires a high score in assessments (such as Mastery Learning), have such a positive effect-size. If we have made sure the student has retained at least 80% of the early learning, their capacity to learn new material is significantly increased.

Short-term memory

There is a clear distinction between Working Memory, which lasts a few seconds and is very limited, and long-term memory, which last for years and has near-infinite capacity. So what about the things we remember for a short time? What sort of memory is it when we first decide what we want to buy and then retain the information while we travel to the shop?

These short-term memories are simply potential long-term memory which have not been repeated enough times to become long-term memory. As with the student in your classroom who seemed to understand the lesson and do the task you set – only to have completely forgotten a few days later.

The synapses have fired, the small gate has opened, the pathway is available, but we have not yet done enough repeats to activate the big gate and form a long-term memory.

This 'forgetting' is very useful to us. If we were to remember all the shopping lists for all the trips we made to the shop in our whole lives, perhaps then our brain would then be full.

ATTENTION AND SELF-REGULATION

Attention is the skill of choosing what is held in Working Memory and then maintaining that focus.

The skill of being able to choose to pay attention to the content of the lesson is vital for learning. This does not mean that the pupil's attention is there constantly, but those with good attention skills can either ignore a distraction or return to the task after it.

The idea of 'paying attention' is very closely linked to the idea of Working Memory as we can say that attention IS what is in Working Memory. As teachers we are all aware that some of our students struggle to pay attention to the lesson and that this significantly reduces their learning.

Attention deficit

There are two learning difficulties associated with this:

ADHD (Attention Deficit Hyperactivity Disorder), where the student is easily distracted and their attention is quickly taken by something else. They act impulsively, shouting out, taking things, hitting someone, etc. When challenged about their behaviour they often cannot answer the question 'Why did you do that?' They don't know because they took the action without thought.

ADD (Attention Deficit Disorder) has no hyperactivity. They may appear shy or wrapped up in their own world.

Self-regulation

AD students do not lack the ability to pay attention – they can often focus well on something that has taken their interest. The difference is they cannot choose what to pay attention to – they are carried away with their own thoughts of what the person next to them just said, etc. They cannot self-regulate. They cannot choose to pay attention to the lesson.

One way to help these students is to reduce the number of distractors as much as possible. We will look at this in more detail in the first part of Section 2 which sets the environment for learning.

Delayed gratification

Closely linked to attention is 'delayed gratification' – the ability to wait until later for the positive outcome of the action we are taking now. This is the opposite of 'impulsivity', which is the habit of seeking gratification immediately.

Success in education (and many other aspects of adult life) is dependent on delayed gratification:

- The work we do now, gets us the exam result later.
- The money we save now gets us the deposit on a house years later.

There is a famous test which illustrates this – the Marshmallow Test. Young children are put in a room alone with a single marshmallow on a plate. They are told that if, when the adult returns, the marshmallow is uneaten, they will be given two. If they eat the marshmallow, they get no more. There are some lovely YouTube videos of children doing this test.

The more interesting aspect educationally is that children who can delay gratification aged 5 do better in a wide range of aspects of adult life:

■ Better career prospects
■ Longer-term relationships
■ Less likely to end up in prison
■ Less likely to be addicted to drugs or alcohol, etc.

Self-regulation in the brain

What is happening (or not happening!) in the brain when someone is self-regulating and choosing what to pay attention to?

Brain research shows that the brain isn't a single thing. It is a collection of functional areas, some relatively primitive (we share them with reptiles) and some more recent (shared just with mammals or even only with humans). Figure 3.12 illustrates how three brain regions work together.

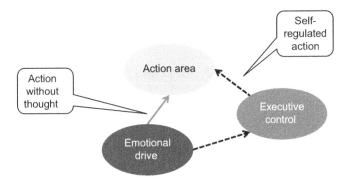

FIGURE 3.12

Our emotional drives come from a primitive part of the brain near the centre. We take action in another primitive area called the motor cortex (marked as 'Action area'). Just above our eyes is an area which is most highly developed in humans – the central Executive. We use this area to override our natural instincts and decide whether an action is appropriate.

When we take action instinctively (the solid grey arrow), a message is sent from the emotion centre to the motor cortex which then signals the muscles to act – run, hit, grab, shout, submit, etc. The links are immediate. We are all born like that and only develop self-regulation as we grow.

The self-regulated action (the dashed arrows) is controlled by the Executive and is about 10× slower than the instinctive response. These areas mature by about age 25.

People with Attention Deficit have weak Executive control. When challenged about their behaviour they sometimes struggle to explain why they acted like that. This is because it was not a conscious decision. Drugs used to control AD are stimulants which activate the Executive pathways and allow the student to be more self-controlled; thinking before acting. To prevent drug dependency, the self-control pathways need to be practised while using the drug. They will then become stronger and the student can reduce their Attention Deficit (and any drug-taking).

We can see the opposite effect when normally self-regulating adults have drunk too much alcohol. The alcohol dulls the Executive pathways while leaving the instinctive pathways intact. People perform amazingly uninhibited actions while drunk which they often feel embarrassed about when sober.

DIFFERENT BRAINS OR LEARNING DIFFICULTIES?

All brains have a different balance of skills and there is sometimes a trade-off so that students with a 'learning difficulty' may also have enhanced skills in another area.

Besides ADD and ADHD, teachers will regularly encounter some other 'learning difficulties':

- Dyslexia (word blindness): difficulty with reading and spelling.
- Dyscalculia (number blindness): difficulty with number.
- Autistic Spectrum (mind blindness): difficulty knowing what another person is thinking or feeling.

What neuroscience reveals is that all brains are different. We do not have a 'reading area', a 'maths area', and so on. Instead, the brain has quite a number of specialist areas – sight, hearing, movement, touch, self-regulation, speech forming, Working Memory, etc. Every individual has a different balance of strengths in these areas. However, we sometimes make the mistake of thinking that these are fixed characteristics – like hair colour, height, etc. What brain research shows is that, even after a stroke, most people's brains are sufficiently plastic to enable them to re-learn a lost skill.

This means that, while someone who 'has dyslexia' will always find more difficulty with reading than most, they can still improve their reading skills with practice. The learning will just take longer.

A further problem of dividing students into 'normal' and 'learning difficulty' groups is that we can ignore all those students who, for instance, are struggling to read and spell, but who do not score badly enough to be given a 'diagnosis' and hence get the extra help they need.

Much better to identify all students who are struggling to read and help them all.

Disorder or difference?

We sometimes make the situation worse by using labels like 'disorder', 'syndrome', etc. or as 'having a learning difficulty'.

If someone is described as 'He has dyslexia', 'She suffers from Asperger's syndrome', etc., it gives the impression there is something wrong with them. While some people do 'suffer', the majority are unaware that they have a 'problem' until someone tells them so.

We can simply refer to them as differences. All the brains of our students are different. They all have different balances of skills and potentials. We just identify some students who are struggling with an aspect of learning and call them by a negative name.

Some people have asked why evolution has allowed these 'learning difficulties' to persist in the population. If they are so harmful, surely the 'survival of the fittest' should have eliminated this trait. However, we can see that sometimes these types of brain have advantages.

Some dyslexic people are better are visualising things and seeing the 'big picture'. They may become architects, designers, entrepreneurs or engineers.

Those with Attention Deficit have difficulty following a plan. This means they have to try new ways of doing things. Occasionally, some come up with a better way of doing things. Other 'neurotypical' people see this and try it out. The tribe benefits.

People with autistic tendencies can find social situations challenging, but some can focus on one thing for an extended period. They are not distracted by office gossip, for instance. This makes them better-than-average at jobs which require attention to detail.

DEVELOPING THE 'THEORY OF LEARNING'

At the end of Chapter 2, on evidence, we started to demonstrate how, if we arrange the effective methods into the order the learner needs to encounter them in order to maximise their learning, we start to create a shared understanding of the learning process. What it lacked at that stage was an explanation before we could call it a 'Theory of Learning'.

This section has provided that explanation and we can now be more confident that, if we now look at individual methods in more detail, we will be applying this 'learning theory' and our students will benefit.

These brain-based explanations make our 'Theory of Learning' more secure because, if we find that a part of the evidence from Hattie, Rosenshine or neuroscience is not quite correct, it no longer matters as much as it did in the past. The 'Theory of Learning' no longer relies on individual bits of evidence being perfect; it now depends on the overall pattern of the evidence.

An analogy

When Charles Darwin was on the *Beagle*, he started to amass evidence which later became part of his 'Theory of Evolution'. Perhaps, when he was writing *Origin of Species* he relied on a piece of evidence which, in later years, was shown to be false. Would this disprove the theory? Obviously not; by then, much more evidence had been gathered which supported the theory.

IT ISN'T ABOUT TEACHERS WORKING HARDER

Because these methods are more effective, you should be able to achieve either:

- The same results for your students with a lower workload or
- Better results with no extra workload for you, the teacher

To achieve these benefits you will need to be sure you are taking your students through the Learning Cycle. The next Section goes through the individual methods in more detail, showing how you can apply them in your classroom.

FURTHER READING

Chartered College of Teaching (2020) Impact No. 8: *Cognition and learning.*
Churches et al. (2017) *Neuroscience for Teachers.* Crown House.
Drommett et al. (2011) Learning and the brain. Teachers' Pocketbooks.

2

EFFECTIVE CLASSROOM PRACTICE

INTRODUCTION

In Section 1 we looked at: finding reliable evidence, what the evidence shows about the most effective teaching methods, how the evidence can be arranged into five major steps and how brain science can help provide explanations for effectiveness.

Section 2 takes you through the Five Steps of the Learning Cycle and shows how each method can be applied.

The Five Steps are:

1. Checking and repairing **Prior Knowledge.**
2. Effective ways to **Present** new information.
3. How to set a **Challenging Task** to promote the learning process.
4. Ways to provide **Feedback for Improvement** so that the correct memories are being formed.
5. Ways to offer **Spaced Repetition** to ensure long-term memories are formed.

As we saw in Chapter 3, learning consists of making new long-term pathways between brain cells. The pathways should always connect to previous memories.

This means that, from the brain's perspective, the Learning Cycle looks more like this:

1. **Prior Knowledge:** Ensure there is something to connect to.
2. **Presentation:** Initiate the pathway.

3. **Challenging Task:** Activate the pathway.
4. **Feedback for Improvement:** Check that it's the right pathway.
5. **Spaced Repetition:** Secure long-term connections by re-using the pathway over a period of time.

This means that it is not so much the individual teaching methods that are important; it is whether the student has been taken through the Learning Cycle.

If you use the Learning Cycle to identify where improvement is needed, you may decide that the problem is Prior Knowledge and that your Presentation skills are fine. In this case you can leave Chapter 5 for now and just focus on Chapter 4.

Remember that the Learning Cycle also applies to your own learning of a new method. You will need a little study, feedback and repetition to master the method, so don't try too much at a time. It is actually harder for an experienced teacher to become proficient with a new method than it is for a beginner. This is because the connections for the new learning are initially much weaker than those of your current method, so that longer practice is needed to get to the point where the new method is part of your everyday practice.

At the end of each method you will find about three sources of Further Reading. If possible, use one or more of these (or another source) to read around the method before trying it.

This section does not cover every known effective method; we have simply included methods which appear on more than one of the lists created by our five main sources (see Chapter 2).

4

Prior Knowledge

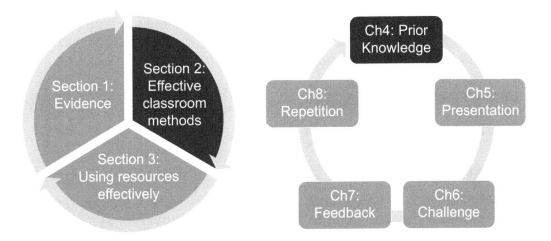

Prior Knowledge Quiz

True or false? *(Answers on p. 154)*

1. Long-term memories are formed by repetitions.
2. Long-term memory and Working Memory work in similar ways.
3. Memories in the brain are similar to memories on a computer.

OVERVIEW

The evidence shows that new learning can only be built on existing, prior knowledge if it is to be understood. You will need to Identify the Prior Knowledge needed for the topic you are about to teach, assess your pupils and make significant efforts to fill in the missing links.

Case study: Yr 10 Science

Mr F is teaching a middle-ability, Yr 10 science group about in-vitro fertilisation (test-tube babies).

He is starting lesson 2 on the topic, but soon becomes aware of the blank faces in the room and that the students were asking the type of question which showed they had not understood most of the previous lesson.

Mr F asked probing questions which revealed that none of the students knew anything about sexual reproduction in plants, a topic they had covered in Yr 8. Without the basic ideas of male and female sex cells joining, multiplying etc. there was little chance they could understand the human, test-tube example.

We look at Prior Knowledge from formal education and from everyday life and include the idea of vocabulary as Prior Knowledge which may need to be repaired if your students are to access your lesson.

TYPES OF PRIOR KNOWLEDGE

There are two types of Prior Knowledge.

In-topic Prior Knowledge

The first is the in-topic knowledge you hope the student has retained from earlier lessons on the topic or earlier learning on the subject. If your topic will be covered in 12 lessons, then, in lesson 3, Prior Knowledge includes the material covered in lessons 1 and 2.

This Prior Knowledge is easier to identify because, as the teacher, you will be aware of the material you have covered.

Pre-topic Prior Knowledge

The second, harder type of Prior Knowledge is the knowledge you are assuming the student has when you start to teach the topic. This is not at all easy to know.

In the previous chapter we gave the case study of the teacher who discovers that his students have missing knowledge about the sexual reproduction of plants involving the making of seeds which is preventing them understanding his lesson on test-tube babies. As the plant lessons were several years earlier, he could not know if they had failed to learn about sexual reproduction in plants.

Just as difficult is your students' relevant prior knowledge when you are starting a subject such as Economics, Sociology, Plumbing etc.

where there has been no formal learning before the course. In this case, the only option is to link to everyday knowledge.

In comparing the methods in the Five Steps with common classroom practice it is clear that Prior Knowledge is perhaps the most important part of the Learning Cycle as it is the least understood and the least addressed.

This means that for you to make the most impact on your students' learning, you need to address this issue as a priority.

FROM OUR EVIDENCE SOURCES

Evidence for the importance of Prior Knowledge is contained in several references in the five main research reviews we have used:

- Hattie: *Prior Achievement*
- Hattie and EEF: *Mastery Learning*
- IAE: *Obtain High Success Rate.*

The majority of the evidence relates to ensuring that the current learning is secured before moving on. However, the same evidence applies to Prior Knowledge since the new learning in this lesson becomes the Prior Knowledge for later lessons.

The relevant sections in Hattie's work are titled 'Prior Achievement', but the implications are the same. Hattie's calculation shows this as having an effect-size (ES) of 0.65, which is high. There is a very good link (correlation) between the student's achievement on the current topic and their achievement prior to the topic.

Mastery of an early part of a topic becomes the secure Prior Knowledge for a later part. While 'Mastery Learning' is usually associated with work at the end of the topic to check that the topic material is well learned, it equally applies to our assessment of Prior Knowledge before a topic starts.

The Education Endowment Foundation (EEF) defines Mastery Learning as follows:

> Traditional teaching keeps time spent on a topic constant and allows pupils' 'mastery' of curriculum content to vary. Mastery learning keeps learning outcomes constant but varies the time needed for pupils to become proficient or competent at these objectives.

> Mastery learning breaks subject matter and learning content into units with clearly specified objectives which are pursued until they are achieved. Learners work through each block of content in a series of sequential steps and must demonstrate a high level of success on tests, typically about 80%, before progressing to the

next unit. Those who do not reach the required level are provided with additional tuition, peer support, small group discussions, or homework, so that they can reach the expected level. (EEF Toolkit)

The purpose of Mastery is to ensure that the learning has taken place before moving on precisely because new learning has to be linked to Prior Knowledge.

Rosenshine also reports the evidence in a similar way, but using the term 'Obtain high success rate'. Obtaining an 80% pass-rate before moving on has been shown to significantly improve learning.

Again and again in the evidence we see the effectiveness of methods, which aim to ensure that the learning has taken place before we move on: spaced practice, one-to-one tuition, quizzes and homework are all methods found in the reviews to ensure that the foundation for the next learning has happened.

EVIDENCE FROM SUPPORTING SOURCES

There are further significant references in the supporting material:

The Coalition for Psychology in Schools and Education Principle 2 states: 'What students already know affects their learning'.

> *Students come to classrooms with knowledge based on their everyday experiences, social interactions, intuitions, and what they have been taught in other settings and in the past. This prior knowledge affects how they will incorporate new learning because what students already know interacts with the material being learned. Accordingly, learning consists of either adding to existing student knowledge, known as conceptual growth, or transforming or revising student knowledge, known as conceptual change. (CPSE 2015)*

Principle 1 from the Institute for Teaching (IfT) is: 'What do students already know?' They offer a helpful analogy:

> *Learning new knowledge is like adding bricks when building a wall. If bricks are missing lower down the wall, the foundations are insecure and the wall will collapse. (IfT 2018)*

Neuroscience for Teachers explains that because memories are connections in the brain:

> *When you plan and organise learning activities, make sure there is plenty of opportunity for the children to make connections between the ideas and knowledge you have presented and other concepts they have learned. (Churches 2017)*

With all these sources, we can be confident that time spent on Prior Knowledge will be time well spent towards raising achievement.

SPOTTING MISSING PRIOR KNOWLEDGE IN YOUR CLASSROOM

Here are some suggestions for ways to spot missing Prior Knowledge in your classroom:

- You have explained the same thing more than once and the student still does not understand.
- The student asks you a question which seems unconnected with the topic.
- Several students ask you the same question and your answer contains something you assumed they already knew.

EXAMPLES OF MISSING PRIOR KNOWLEDGE

Here is a case study from a real classroom of a teacher who has noticed that their student's lack of progress is a Prior Knowledge problem (rather than ability, effort etc.).

Case study: Yr 10 Science

Mr B is tutoring a 16-year-old female student who is struggling with her science. She is scoring D and E grades in GCSE assessments but wants B grade for entry to A-level courses.

Mr B is initially sceptical, but soon discovers that she was quite able and, indeed, understands some quite difficult ideas in chemistry and physics.

Making little progress with Chemistry, Mr B starts one session with a list of basic Chemistry words: atom, element, compound, mixture, crystal, bond, etc. Suddenly the problem reveals itself; she was unsure of the meaning of nearly all these words!

Over the summer break they ignore course material and concentrate only on basics; learning about atoms, compounds, elements, etc. The following term the student has a Chemistry assessment. As they had been working on Prior Knowledge, they have not been revising the material for the test, so she is almost embarrassed by coming top of the class.

Once the Prior Knowledge was in place, her brain simply reconnected all the difficult material she had learned by rote earlier and her 'understanding' blossomed.

She gets her B grade.

BRAIN-BASED EXPLANATION

We know that memories are links. In the example of the student with missing Chemistry knowledge, the better understanding she develops can be represented (much simplified) by the diagram of links in Figure 4.1. This is sometimes referred to as a 'schema'.

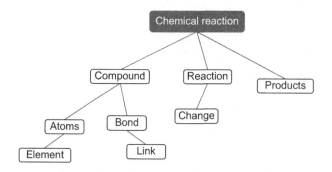

FIGURE 4.1

In Figure 4.2 we see the effect of trying to learn new material with and without secure Prior Knowledge. The white dots and lines represent the new material, while the black ones represent the Prior Knowledge. In the left diagram the links to Prior Knowledge (dashed grey lines) cannot be made as the Prior Knowledge is partly missing. Although it is possible to learn the material, it will not make sense, and so may simply be rote, or inflexible learning.

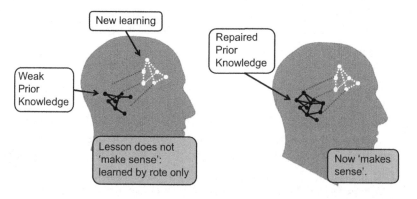

FIGURE 4.2

Once the vital, missing Prior Knowledge has been learned (as on the right diagram), the rote learning now makes sense and is integrated into the student's schema for chemical reactions. She now 'understands' it.

ASSESSING PRIOR KNOWLEDGE

Knowing what your students need to know before they start your course is by no means easy. This is sometimes called the 'curse of knowledge'. Because we are familiar with the material, it is difficult for us to see the learning through the eyes of the learner.

Some teachers are lucky. The course materials contain some suitable material.

Ms V told us:

> We use a textbook which very helpfully says 'What you have learnt before' at the start of a new topic. I check the key points and make up some multiple choice questions to test knowledge and understanding of these areas. Hinge Point-style questions are really useful here.

> I also use examiners' reports to highlight common misconceptions and always highlight these when teaching.

Developing your own initial, Prior Knowledge assessment

If Prior Knowledge is as essential as the research suggests it is (that, literally, no-one can learn anything if they cannot link it to something they already know), then it is worth putting time and effort into developing the pre-assessment material. Because it is hard to identify the Prior Knowledge just by 'thinking about' it, you probably need something more systematic.

The best ways to develop the materials for this is to work collaboratively with other teachers of that topic.

- Brainstorm: ask the group 'What knowledge (including vocabulary) do the students need to access this topic?'
- Logic: Look at the new material and ask yourself what they will need to know.
- Listen to students' questions and note down any which are often asked.

Students are always asking questions about things they do not understand. If only one or two students ask a question which shows they have not understood something, then explain it to them (or ask them further questions to try to understand where exactly they have not understood). If, however, you hear the same question again and again, or if you realise this question comes up every time you start this topic, then this reveals a Prior Knowledge problem.

FILLING IN MISSING PRIOR KNOWLEDGE

This will often require that you change the way the topic is taught. Unless you do a Prior Knowledge assessment and repair process already, you need to invent one and give time to implement it.

Case study: Yr 3 Maths

Mr N is teaching Maths to Yr 3. The objective is for students to be able to tell the time to the nearest 5 mins, but, when assessed, many students make mistakes, mixing up 'quarter to' and 'quarter past', for example.

Mr N revisits the topic, but this time focusses just on 'past' times until those are secure before moving on to 'to' times. Later he reassesses the class and many more students show understanding.

Case study: English as a Second Language

Mr A is helping a Romanian student who has weak English on how to make nouns plurals. He finds the student is struggling because she does not know the words themselves! Mr A gets her to empty her pencil case. They spend the session learning the words 'pen', 'pencil', etc. *and* the plurals.

Do I have time for this?

When we first hear this, our immediate response may be that such a process was impossible as we hardly have time to cover the course material anyway.

However, when we see the high effect-size of applying the evidence we realise that, even if we took several lessons to cover Prior Knowledge, we actually end up with more time, as the students simply learn faster! As with the student in the Case study above with missing GCSE Chemistry Prior Knowledge, sometimes filling in Prior Knowledge allows a whole lot of learning which the student cannot 'make sense' of, to become linked and so become accessible as new learning.

Sometimes doing a Prior Knowledge assessment saves you time. Sometimes the students are more advanced than you thought.

Case study

Mr H is teaching an able Yr 8 group about 'Earth and Space'. In the first lesson he notices several high-level questions from the students. He decides to do an assessment using the topic revision questions usually used before the end-of-topic test. The students score between 60% and 90%! Mr H identifies the questions which most students got wrong and focusses on that material. The topic takes 5 lessons rather than the usual 12.

Sometimes we are aware the student already knows the material, but we spend time on it anyway!

Case study
Ms T is a staff trainer at a Further Education college. She is observing a gym instructor taking a student through the various machines in the gym, using them to see what she already knows.
Despite finding that she is fluent on all the machines, he proceeds to teach her about each machine again. When challenged by Ms T afterwards, the instructor defends the re-teaching: 'Well, it was on my session plan, so I needed to do that'.

Make use of your assessment; don't stick to your plan

As the lists show, there is no one way to teach well. The lists of effective methods we use here were created from experiments where a particular method is tried out on students. Another approach would be to look in the classrooms of highly successful teachers and see if there are common factors. Unfortunately, when this has been tried, no general patterns emerged as there are so many ways to be successful.

One common feature stood out, however: successful teachers rarely stuck to their lesson plan! While less effective teachers may 'plough on', the most successful teachers continuously monitor the learning of their students and adjust the teaching accordingly. It's a bit like a ship's captain, who knows the destination, but monitors their position, and adjusts their course to respond to wind and tide.

Repairing Prior Knowledge and the Learning Cycle

Although 'Filling missing knowledge' is just one step in the Learning Cycle, it needs to be approached by applying the whole Learning Cycle. The material needs to be presented in the most effective ways, we need to set the students tasks which challenge them, they need feedback to make an improvement and they need repetition over time.

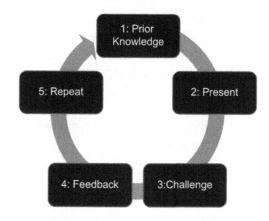

FIGURE 4.3

These vital steps are spelled out in the coming chapters.

Evidence for repairing missing knowledge

Looking back to the five research reviews we are using as evidence sources, we see a range of techniques which can be used to help repair Prior Knowledge.

The EEF list includes:

- One-to-one tuition
- Peer tutoring
- Small-group tuition.

The interesting connection between these three is the size of the group. Unless you have identified a widespread missing Prior Knowledge with your class (which means you can do the repair work with the whole group), smaller groups work best.

The research shows that, while one-to-one tuition has the highest effect-size, it is also the most expensive. However, we get very similar results with a group of three students and the value of the small group only starts to diminish significantly when the group is above five.

As we will see again in Section 3, on using Teaching Assistants effectively, the best use of your resources is not to have someone sit with the pupil in the lesson, it is to give them small-group or individual tuition outside the classroom with someone trained to assess and repair that type of Prior Knowledge.

WHEN SHOULD I USE THIS METHOD IN MY CLASSROOM?

By definition, Prior Knowledge needs to be assessed before you start teaching the new material. You also need to give time for any repair exercises you identify.

PUTTING THESE METHODS INTO ACTION

- Choose a topic you will be teaching shortly afterwards.
- Using the textbook or course outline, identify the main learning for the topic.
- Put yourself in the place of the learner and ask 'What would I need to know to understand this new material?'
- Get a group of teachers together who have taught (or are about to teach) this topic and ask them the same question. (Often a dialogue produces better results than just thinking in isolation.)
- Ask yourself and the other teachers to remember things which students often get wrong or questions they often ask.
- Design a pre-topic assessment for your group. Give the assessment to the class as far in advance as possible. This gives time for you to plan the 'repair' process.
- Plan 'repair' lessons for the whole class if widespread Prior Knowledge is missing or small-group interventions for individuals if the proportion is smaller.
- While you are teaching the topic, note down areas where students regularly fail to learn or questions which are often asked. Add this to your Prior Knowledge file for the next time you teach this topic.

Of course, you will never be able to meet all the needs of all the students. Some will have good Prior Knowledge and be bored while you go over it for the others. Some may need more support than you are able to offer. However, overall, the learning on the topic will be enhanced significantly. The evidence shows we can be confident that your time and effort will be worth it.

VOCABULARY AS PRIOR KNOWLEDGE

Case study
Ms C is teaching a boy who is struggling with the text. The boy explains that he does not know the meaning of a certain word in the paragraph they are using. Ms C explains the meaning, but then asks him to highlight all the words in the paragraph of which

he did not know the meaning. She comes back a few minutes later and is shocked to see he had highlighted the majority of the non-simple words.

It is not just with low-achieving students that there can be problems. This case study concerns high-achieving A-level students.

Case study: A-level English

Mr R is teaching Shakespeare's play *Othello* to A-level students. He finds he cannot rely on them to read and understand the language. There is so much vocabulary they do not know, and so many words which have multiple meanings. He gets the students to read the text and then underline the words they do not know or are confused by.

He then clarifies the word-meanings before moving onto the text itself.

As teachers, we are often aware of the need for our students to know the meaning of the keywords and technical terms they have learned in previous lessons. However, we are less aware of the need to ensure they understand the ordinary vocabulary we are using.

Teachers who try this exercise with their students (at any level) report experiences similar to those of the teacher in the Case study above: they are generally amazed at how many ordinary words their students do not know.

Let's look again at an earlier paragraph as heard by a student with limited vocabulary.

As teachers, we are often xxxxxx of the need for our students to know the meaning of the keywords and xxxxxxxx they have learned in previous lessons. However, we are less xxxxxx of the need to xxxxxx they understand the ordinary xxxxxxxxx we are using.

The sentence makes no sense to them.

Case study: Yr 7 Science

Mr D is teaching a Yr 7 class. In the first unit test, a boy who he had rated as in the top third of ability (from his classroom interactions) was scoring in the bottom third. When this happens again, he looks more closely at the test papers. Mr D sees that the boy's answers are quite high-level – it's just they are not answers to the actual question! He discusses this with the student and discovers that he did not know the meanings of some ordinary words (his technical word knowledge was good) and so had, without realising it, guessed what the question meant.

The boy's mother tells Mr D that the boy loves sport, but does little reading. Mr D decides to work with the parent and gives her a list of the most common words in English. The boy and his mother go through the lists, deleting all the words he already knows. Over the next months they practice the unknown words (often on the way to and from sports fixtures). By the end of the academic year the boy is scoring much higher, as he is now answering the actual question!

Assessing your students' vocabulary

One way to check vocabulary for the topic you are teaching is to give your students a text from the topic. This could be the textbook or something you have written yourself for use in this topic. Ask them to highlight the words they do not know/understand. Then identify the most common unknown words and teach them directly, using homework and repeated, spaced testing to secure the words in long-term memory.

There are a variety of ways to assess vocabulary, of which a few are listed here. (This book aims to give the big picture of 'what works' in education, so we do not go into detail about vocabulary). There are also several excellent resources available.

Quiz to check understanding

True or false? *(Answers on p. 157)*

1. New learning does not need to be linked to Prior Knowledge.
2. Missing Prior Knowledge is a serious impediment to learning.
3. Vocabulary is Prior Knowledge for all learning, so vocabulary checks and repair are vital.
4. Phonics is Prior Knowledge for reading.
5. You do not have time to repair Prior Knowledge.

REFERENCE LIST AND FURTHER READING

GENERAL PRIOR KNOWLEDGE

Ceri Dean. (2012) *Classroom Instruction That Works*. Ch 4: Cues, questions and Advance Organisers.

Institute for Educational Sciences. (2007) *Organizing Instruction and Study to Improve Student Learning*. Recommendation 5a: Use pre-questions to introduce a new topic.

Barak Rosenshine. (2012) *Principles of Instruction*. Principle 1: Daily review.

VOCABULARY

Isabel L. Beck. (2013) *Bringing Words to Life*. Guilford Press.
Alex Quigley. (2018) *Closing the Vocabulary Gap*. Routledge.

METHODS FOR FILLING IN MISSING KNOWLEDGE

Education Endowment Foundation. *Toolkit*: One-to-one tuition; Peer tutoring; Small group tuition.

5

Presenting new material

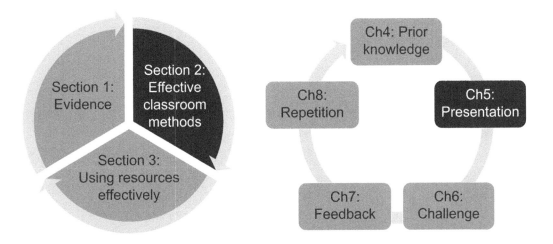

This chapter includes five methods, or things to consider when presenting new material to your students.

Of course, you will continue to use your current methods, but these are five ways which, the evidence shows, enhance learning (and so make your job easier).

IN SUMMARY

1. Recognising the **Working Memory limit** ensures that you do not overload your students with too much new information at one time.

2. **Linking to Prior Knowledge** helps students make connections which lead to good long-term memories.

3. Using a **Multi-sensory** approach means you make better use of parts of your students' brains for learning.
4. Giving your students an **Advance Organiser** helps them see the big picture of your topic as you teach the detail.
5. **Linking Abstract Ideas to Concrete Examples** is an effective way to enable students to understand the more difficult ideas you teach.

FURTHER READING

Allison and Tharby. (2015) *Making Every Lesson Count*. Ch 2: Explanation.
Geoff Petty. (2018) *Teach Even Better*. Ch 8: Presenting new content to students.

METHOD 1: WORKING MEMORY LIMIT

Prior Knowledge quiz

True or false. *(Answers on p. 154)*

1. Most students can store around seven items in their Working Memory.
2. Working Memory capacity changes with age, with the peak reached in mid-teens.
3. All students of the same age have the same Working Memory capacity.
4. Having good Long-Term Memories frees up Working Memory space.

Overview

This case study illustrates one of the ways that the Working Memory limit arises in your classroom.

Case study

Ms J is teaching a mixed-ability group. She gives them some instructions and more than half the class get started. She notices that Sian hasn't started. She asks: 'What's the problem, Sian?' Sian looks up a bit confused. 'What are we doing?' Ms J gives a kindly smile, repeats the instruction and says 'Make sure you're listening next time'.

A few minutes later, Jane sees that Sian has still not started. She gives her a firm look. Sian immediately starts asking other students what they need to do. She starts copying from Steven.

But is Ms J right? Was Sian simply 'not listening'? Perhaps she simply doesn't have enough space in her Working Memory to store all the information Ms J was giving.

We all have a limit to the number of different things we can 'think about' at once. If we don't recognise the limits and present too much new information at a time, our students will be easily overloaded and not able to take in what they are trying to learn.

Applying the Working Memory limit approach is about judging how much new information we deliver in one go and planning how to break down the topic into smaller chunks.

Once some of the new material is in your students' long-term memory, it takes up less space in Working Memory and hence you can move forward.

About Working Memory limit

You may notice that Working Memory limit is only identified by one of the five evidence sources we have used. It is included here because it is so strongly supported by cognitive neuroscience.

Working Memory is the space in the brain where we store thoughts and images for a few seconds, while we think about something. It is separate from long-term, permanent memories. The diagram below shows how they are connected.

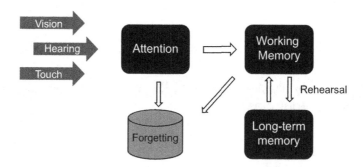

FIGURE 5.1

In practical terms the average adult Working Memory capacity is about 7 items with a range of 5–9. This capacity is fully developed by about 15 years, so younger students have lower capacity.

Working Memory is made up of two main components:

- The auditory loop: where we repeat some words in our head.
- The visual-spatial sketchpad: where we store images we're thinking of.

A fuller explanation of Working Memory can be found in Chapter 3:

Let's compare the experience of two students in your classroom. Student 1 has an average Working Memory of seven spaces, while Student 2 has only five spaces. Although, as a teacher, we know not to give too much information in one go, we generally just intuit how much to give from our own experience.

Figure 5.2 shows what Student 1 experiences. They hear the whole task and are able to act on it.

1	2	3	4	5	6	7
Collect pen	and paper.	Write the date	and title	at the top.	Do Q 4	on page 65

FIGURE 5.2

Unfortunately, Figure 5.3 shows that student 2 has a different experience. The first five parts of the instruction fill their Working Memory, but the teacher keeps going! The rest of the instruction overwrites part of their Working Memory. When they now reflect on the task, they have a near-nonsense instruction.

1	2	3	4	5
~~Collect pen~~ Do Q 4	~~and paper.~~ on page 65	Write the date	and title	at the top.

FIGURE 5.3

As Student 2 doesn't know what to do, he just sits there. He's had this experience before in other lessons. To him, 'not knowing what to do' is a normal part of his experience. He probably knows that, sooner or later, the teacher will come round and help, or his classmate will explain, or perhaps he will just sit there.

As the teacher we may become frustrated. We have seen Student 2 do this before. We get annoyed. 'Why weren't you listening, I just explained it! Look! Student 1 is doing as I asked! For heaven's sake, boy, pay attention'.

Analogy

You are collecting the ingredients for a meal at the supermarket, or collecting the tools you need for that DIY job at home. Your bag is big enough to carry the ingredients or tools. You arrive back to do the task, unpack the ingredients or tools and start the job.

However, what happens if the bag you take is too small? Some of the ingredients or tools will need to be left behind and, when you start, you cannot do the job as vital ingredients or tools are missing.

This is how one of our evidence sources explains it:

> Our working memory, the place where we process information, is small. It can only handle a few bits of information at once – too much information swamps our working memory. Presenting too much material at once may confuse students because their short-term memory will be to process it.

The more-successful teachers … only presented small amounts of new material at one time, and they taught in such a way that each point was mastered before the next point was introduced. They checked their students' understanding on each point and re-taught material when necessary.

Cognitive load theory

This is a fancy name for the same thing. There is an extensive literature on this with good advice for teachers. You will find some of the basic ideas here. Once you are familiar with these basics you may like to extend your knowledge on Working Memory by further reading.

Reducing demand on Working Memory

Write down the instructions

Ms T is teaching a Yr 5 class. She finds that, if she simply gives them verbal instructions, some students sit there looking at the page, confused as to what they are doing. She now makes sure the instructions are written down and only gives them one or two items at a time.

Teach in smaller chunks

At one level we are all aware of the Working Memory limit. We never teach all the material in the topic in one go. We always break it down into smaller chunks. But:

- How did you decide how much new information to give the class this lesson?
- What made you decide that more would be too much?

If you spot that the learning is being limited by Working Memory capacity, consciously decide to reduce the amount of new material presented at one time.

Case study: Yr 3 English
Mr W is teaching the use of 'speech marks' in English to Yr 3. Having introduced the idea that they are only used around the words someone says, he sets them the task of writing a paragraph which includes speech marks.

He soon discovers that the idea is not well understood. One student has put speech marks around the whole paragraph.

Another has put the opening marks, but then forgotten. He realises that they are more interested in their story than in the task.

He now gives them practice, starting with exercises where they need to put the speech marks into sentences which he provides for them. He gradually moves them onto the harder tasks when they are more secure in their use of speech marks.

Case study: Yr 1 Learning to read
Ms L has found that, when learning to read, while sounding out the words, some students lose track of the meaning of the sentence. She now gets them to sound out a few words and then has the student go back and read the sentence so far. When they finally complete the sentence, she gets them to read the whole of it.

Link to Prior Knowledge

As we saw in the section on Working Memory in Chapter 3, if we can use links from long-term memory we can save space. This means knowing what Prior Knowledge your students have as long-term memories (as in the previous chapter). This is another example which illustrates that learning is not maximised by the teacher knowing which methods are most effective and using some of them, it is maximised by the teacher understanding the learning process as a whole.

Habits and routines

We can create Prior Knowledge by establishing routines in the classroom. These will become stored as long-term memories and hence save space. In the example above, if 'Collect pen and paper. Write the date and title at the top' is used often and is a routine in long-term memory, it will only occupy one space in Working Memory, leaving the rest of the space for other instructions or thinking.

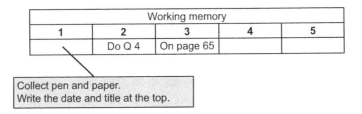

FIGURE 5.4

Reducing distractions

We can design the classroom to optimise Working Memory load. In brief: try to de-clutter the physical space you are teaching from so that your student is not distracted and can focus only on what they need to learn. We may have the impression that having this week's keywords or some student work around the board area will help. However, if these take up Working Memory space while your student is trying to attend to the board/screen, then less space is available to process the lesson material.

1	2	3	4	5	6	7
Space available for learning					Space taken by distraction	

FIGURE 5.5

Notice what your students are getting distracted by and try to eliminate it. For example, they may be distracted by something out of the window or through the window in the door. Try some diffusing material which lets the light in, but does not give a clear view.

Using both types of Working Memory

Since we have both auditory and visual types of Working Memory, it makes sense to use both. We expand on this idea later in this chapter: Multi-sensory approach.

When should I use this method in my classroom?

The short answer is: bear this in mind whenever you are presenting new information, giving instructions, etc. If you overload their Working Memory and your communication fails, it is not their fault.

Many of the methods in this book are ways to teach your students. 'Working Memory limit' is not so much a method as something you need to bear in mind whenever you are teaching anyone anything. It is so easy to overload the student (or friend, colleague, customer, etc.).

Putting these methods into action

When planning your teaching, look at the new material you will be teaching in that unit and consciously decide how to divide it with Working Memory in mind.

If you have chosen well you will find that most students gain the new knowledge/skill/understanding. Simply help the others and keep up the pace.

If, however, you notice that many students don't 'get it', first decide if the problem is missing Prior Knowledge. If it is, deal with that first. If not, try smaller 'chunks' and the types of skills practice shown in the Case Studies discussed previously.

Quiz to check understanding

True or false. *(Answers on p. 157)*

1. Having a decorated area around the board helps students learn.
2. All students have the same amount of Working Memory.
3. Rote learning frees up space in Working Memory.

FURTHER READING

Churches et al. (2017) *Neuroscience for Teachers*. Ch2: Learning and remembering.

Barak Rosenshine. (2012) *Principles of Instruction*. Principle 2: Present new material using small steps.

METHOD 2: LINKING TO PRIOR KNOWLEDGE

Prior Knowledge quiz

True or false? *(Answers on p. 155)*

1. Prior Knowledge is important, but not vital to learning.
2. Prior Knowledge is what the student has learned in previous lessons on this topic.
3. New long-term memories can be formed instantly.

Need to revise? Look back to Chapter 4: Prior Knowledge and Chapter 3 for an explanation.

Overview

In the previous chapter we looked at the need to identify your students' current Prior Knowledge and to fill in any missing gaps before starting the new material.

We saw that this is important because new knowledge can only be understood if it is linked to what the student already knows.

This method looks at the next step – linking the new material to what the students already know.

Case study

Ms G is teaching Critical Thinking to a Lower 6th, high-ability group. A regular activity is to look at a current newspaper article and discuss it from a 'critical thinking' perspective. Ms G brings a news item about a violent incident between Israelis and Palestinians. Having read the item, she asks the students for their opinion on the article, applying what they have been studying about *reliability of evidence* in news reports.

The students have nothing to say on the topic (whereas they had been engaged in previous, similar activities). It soon transpires that they knew nothing about the topic: not where Israel was, nor that there was a conflict with Palestinians over many years, nor that this area was occupied by Rome at the time of Christ nor about the rise of Islam, etc.

Their lack of Prior Knowledge left them simply unable to engage in any debate about the news item.

About Linking to Prior Knowledge

Types of linking

There are three main situations:

- In-topic links: Making links to the prior learning in the subject or topic.
- New subject links: Making links where the student has no formal learning in the topic.
- Linking abstract ideas to concrete analogies: Making links to abstract ideas which cannot be linked directly to existing knowledge.

In-topic links

If the topic you are about to teach follows on from previous learning in your subject, then the most obvious links you can make are to that previous learning. Of course, you need to be aware of what the Prior Knowledge is that you need to link to. That process has been covered in detail in the previous chapter on Prior Knowledge.

Case study: Science Yr 8

Mr P is about to start a unit on chemical reactions with Yr 8. He wants to know how familiar the students are with the names of elements. He puts a list of the elements he will be using in the chemical reactions in the topic and asks the students to discuss whether they have heard of them before and where.

He finds that some of his students have heard of each of the elements he lists. The classroom discussion also introduces the other students to their names and something about them.

Case study: Spanish

Ms T is about to teach new Spanish words around 'Going on holiday'. She starts by asking the class to write down any words and phrases they already know. She insists on a mix of nouns, verbs and adjectives. Students then discuss their list with a partner.

Students share their lists with the class before Ms T introduces the new material.

New subject links

However, the work you are about to do may have no links from previous lessons. You may be starting to teach a new subject, such as sociology or economics, to students with no formal learning on this subject. In this case, the links you will need to make are to the students' general knowledge or everyday experience.

Case study: City & Guilds NVQ Level 3. Occupational Health and Safety

Ms L found that her usual approach to teaching Health and Safety was met with bored indifference. The ideas she was teaching did not immediately connect with her students' experience.

The next time she taught this topic she tried a different approach. Instead she asked: 'How did you keep healthy and safe on the way to college this morning?' This created a buzz of discussion which got the students' brains connected to what they already knew on the subject.

This secondary History teacher has a similar experience.

Case study: Yr 8 History

Ms H is starting a History topic with Yr 8 on public health in the 19th century. She realises that her students have no direct knowledge of this and so asks the class to come up with things which keep them fit and healthy.

Her students come up with dozens of examples: clean water, vaccinations, medicines, balanced diet, washing, exercise, etc. This process has activated the students' prior knowledge. Ms H then uses these lists to ask whether they would be available to children in the 19th century.

Sometimes the text you plan to use is too far from the students' experience for them to relate to.

Case study: Secondary English

Ms K is teaching English Language with lower-achieving secondary students. She knows that the students can find the usual text pretty dry and they soon lose interest. She reflects on what she was doing that made it so hard for them. They have to access an unseen text and they were finding it really difficult.

She decides to teach the same skills using a different novel: *Stone Cold* by Robert Swindells. This links to their prior knowledge because they can all relate to the central, teenage character and she can use the video backup resource from the BBC.

They enjoyed the story, empathised with the character and had access to non-linguistic, video resources. Ms K found they learned the skills far better than her previous class.

As you may notice in this case study and throughout this book, very often the teacher is using several effective methods at the same time. What this illustrates is that what is important is not so much the individual methods, but the underlying learning process in the mind of the student. The individual methods facilitate parts of that process.

Linking abstract ideas to concrete analogies

This is a special case of linking new material to things the student already knows. Abstract Ideas are ones that cannot be directly experienced through the senses and contrast with 'concrete' ideas which can.

These ideas are developed in more detail in a later part of this chapter.

Why this method works

In a very real, physical sense, new knowledge can only be understood if it can be linked to prior learning. This method applies this to the process of presenting new knowledge to your students.

The more detailed explanation can be found in the previous chapter on Prior Knowledge or in Section 1, Chapter 3 on long-term memories.

When should I use this in my classroom?

As we have seen in the previous chapter, it is vital that new learning is linked to Prior Knowledge. This means that this is very important when starting any new topic or introducing any new idea, particularly an abstract one.

Putting this method into action

Before you can implement this in your lesson, you will need to have carried out Step 1: Checking and Repairing Prior Knowledge. If the Prior Knowledge is not there, your students will not be able to link to it.

This method entails making conscious links with the Prior Knowledge needed for the new material. Phrases like 'Remember when we…' or 'You know that…' help make links.

Quiz to check understanding

True or false. *(Answers on p. 158)*

1. Linking to Prior Knowledge is linking to what you taught them in the previous lesson.
2. Linking to Prior Knowledge makes physical links in the brain of your student to memories they already have.
3. Students will make their own links; you don't need to show them the links.

FURTHER READING

Ceri Dean. (2012) *Classroom Instruction That Works.* Ch 4: Cues, questions and Advance Organisers.

Barak Rosenshine. (2012) *Principles of Instruction.* Principle 1: Daily review.

METHOD 3: MULTI-SENSORY APPROACH

Prior Knowledge quiz

True or false. *(Answers on p. 155)*

1. Students use several senses at a time to access learning.
2. Students have individual 'learning styles' which favour one sense.
3. Some students are weak in processing information from one sense (e.g. hearing)

Overview

We know that memories are simply links in the brain to things already known. The more links we can make, the better the chance of creating new knowledge, linked to existing, prior knowledge.

Taking a multi-sensory approach is a great way to do this. Presenting material both visually and verbally, sometimes referred to as 'dual coding', is proven to help learning.

Note: This is not 'Learning Styles'. All students benefit from a multi-sensory approach.

Use:

- Pictures, diagrams, maps
- Videos, animations and animated slides
- Graphic organisers, including tables and graphs
- Mental images
- Kinaesthetics – gesture and actions
- Physical models.

About a multi-sensory approach

Pictures, diagrams, maps

This is classic 'dual coding'. The students receive the information in two different ways – visual and auditory. However, there are some general rules which help.

Speak to the image. Have very few words on the screen (one suggestion is a maximum of 13 words). Get the students to look at the image and link your speech to the image using some sort of pointer to highlight where you want them to focus.

Note the importance of having very few words on the slide. Almost no-one can read and listen at the same time (because the brain region which interprets 'meaning' is shared between visual (reading) and auditory (hearing). If you also want them to copy text, have this on another slide and try not to talk while they are reading/copying.

Case study: Yr 7 Science

Mr T is giving instructions for a science lesson practical. He has recently heard about 'dual coding': giving information in both word and visual form. In the past he would have written the instructions in words: 'Pour 250 ml into the beaker'.

Now he uses simple cartoon drawings (not high-quality). He draws a beaker and labels it with 250 ml and so cuts down the quantity of written work. He notices that all the students benefit, but especially the slow learners.

Videos, animations and animated slides

A moving visual image can be more effective than a static one, so sometimes videos and animations can be helpful. However, we should not assume, simply because there is a video, we should use it. It needs to comply with what we know about the learning process – so, if, for instance, the video includes too much new material, it will overload Working Memory. If it tries to connect the new learning to things outside the students' knowledge, it will fail.

If you are using computer slides, animate the text: if the material appears on the screen a bit at a time, it can help not to overload Working Memory. For example: if you are presenting a labelled diagram or map, first show the image without labels, then have the labels appear as you introduce them. This doesn't need to be fancy, you don't need to create cartoons!

Graphic Organisers, including tables and graphs

We can get some of the benefits of using graphics, etc. and still use words if we use Graphic Organisers (GO). Essentially, these are words in boxes arranged in some way. Figure 5.6 shows some examples.

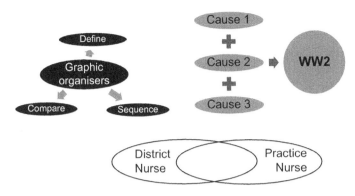

FIGURE 5.6

We only cover Graphical Organisers briefly here because, although they are effective in presenting new information, they are even more effective if your students use them. There is more detail in the following chapter on Challenge.

Tables and graphs are a common form of GO, but we should not assume that they are self-explanatory. If possible, build the GO a bit at a time while running a commentary. 'The column shows… while this one… so, you can see, in this row that …'. 'The bottom axis shows… while the vertical axis shows… So this line shows that…'.

Mental images

Getting your students to construct their own mental images also helps. If they close their eyes while you tell a story they can 'see' it in their imagination. We get similar benefits to 'dual coding' as the brain has simultaneously experienced both auditory and visual material.

Kinaesthetics – gesture and actions

Use arm gestures yourself to highlight aspects of the learning and get your students to act out aspects of what they are learning. They can be atoms in a chemical reaction, volcanoes erupting, soldiers invading, birds flying…

Case study
Ms K is getting her class to revise a topic leading up to an exam. She divides the class into groups of four and gives each group part of the topic. They must produce some images (to be shown on the visualiser), some text (which one student will read while

the images are shown) and some acting to illustrate the point being made.

The class spend one lesson in preparation and another giving their mini-presentations. Many of the presentations are excellent, but Ms K follows them with a short class discussion to clarify important points.

Some presentations are also funny (particularly the kinaesthetic!), so the students gain an emotional component to their memory of the topic.

Remember to keep this additional sensory input in balance. If the play acting is too elaborate then the students may simply remember the acting and not relate it to the intended learning.

Physical models

Although physical objects are common in science lessons, they are less common in other subjects, especially for older students. While Cuisenaire rods, wooden triangles, etc. are common in primary maths lessons, they are often absent in secondary school and above.

Models of castles, chariots, etc. in history, river valleys in geography, etc. are all helpful.

The 3D model is especially helpful to support the 2D diagram you may draw on the board and expect your students to copy. For you the 2D version you are drawing is, in your brain, closely linked to the 3D version in your brain. Don't assume that the diagram they are copying is linking to the same 3D model!

Remember to give your lower-achieving students the chance to touch the models. It's not that they are 'kinaesthetic learners', it's that many are not as good at learning via words.

Case study

Mr L is teaching maths in primary school. He notices that there are still students who are struggling with multiplication and division despite many lessons. He decides to go back to basics and use paper cups.

He places two small tables at the front and puts the cups on one of them.

He asks students to come and move cups onto the 'maths' table. He checks addition learning: 'John, put 3 cups on the maths table'; 'Jane, add 4 more cups'; 'Darren, how many cups do we have now?'; 'So, Emily, when we added 4 cups to 3 cups, what was the result?'

By advancing to multiplication and division over the next few lessons, Mr L manages to create the links between the physical cups and the abstract symbols of number and process.

There is a hierarchy of abstraction. You can bring the thing itself > a model of the thing > a picture > a diagram > just the word.

Case study: French lesson

Ms H is teaching words about 'Food and Drink' to a French language class. She brings in examples of food and drink for the class to see as she introduces the new food/drink words.

Why these methods work

Maximising Working Memory

When we are going to learn something, the information must first be held in our Working Memory. There are two quite separate brain areas: Visual images are initially held in the Visual-Spatial Sketchpad while words are held in the Auditory Loop. This means that new information has twice the chance of getting to Stage 1 in the learning process if it is received using both pathways.

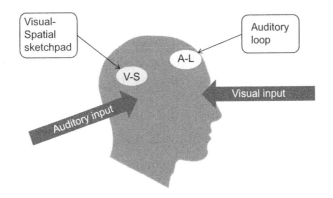

FIGURE 5.7

We know that memories in the brain are links. If we create more links by using more senses (plus emotions) we create better memories. It's not that there is a thing called 'the memory' and that it needs lots of links. The thing we call 'the memory' is just the links, so, a multisensory memory is a better memory by definition.

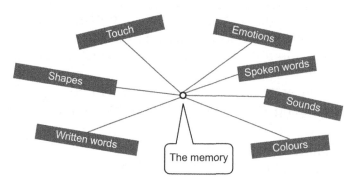

FIGURE 5.8

No, it's not 'Learning Styles'

The idea of 'Learning Styles' is that your students have a preferred way of learning and that, if you teach them in that way, they will learn more quickly. This has been tested several times to a high standard, but no evidence has been found to support the idea.

One common idea is that students are either Visual or Auditory or Kinaesthetic learners (VAK). Although the brain has visual, auditory and kinaesthetic regions, this doesn't mean that students have 'learning styles' or 'learning preferences'. There is no evidence to support these ideas.

Interestingly, in the classic VAK learning styles method, 'A' (auditory) is assumed to include written/read and audible/heard words. However, this makes no sense as hearing words and reading words use separate pathways in the brain. Indeed, many dyslexic readers are excellent listeners and learn well from stories.

So, there is no need to divide (or label) your students with learning styles – just use all the styles with all the students.

When should I use this method in my classroom?

So basic is the idea of using a multi-sensory approach that you should be using it anyway, rather than looking to see if it is a useful tool in your classroom. However, if you are a teacher who predominantly uses verbal and written words, you may well find that you have been labelling some of your low-achieving students as 'low ability' when, in reality, you have been giving them information in too few formats – and that words are not their strong point.

As with almost all these effective methods, they are most effective with lower-achieving students. By definition we call students 'able' or 'gifted' when they respond well to the teaching they have available.

However, we should not conclude that all the others are less able if we are only offering them information in words.

Interestingly, we do have students who have perfectly good hearing, but have weak auditory processing skills and do not understand what they heard. However, we almost never have students with good eyesight, but poor visual processing skills and do not recognise what they have seen. We don't even have a word for it. Consequently, when we use a more visual approach with high-achieving students who were perfectly happy with our 'wordy' teaching, we do not disadvantage them.

We can tell this is the case if we consider advertising, particularly on TV. We almost never see a successful advert with just words on the screen while a voice-over gives different words. We almost always see images which evoke emotions supported by voice-over. If we can reproduce this in our teaching (to some degree) we will be 'selling' our lesson more effectively.

Putting these methods into action

- Pick a topic you will be teaching soon.
- Go through the list of multi-sensory methods and identify which ones you already plan to use.
- Decide whether you are sufficiently multi-sensory.
- If yes, pat yourself on the back. You are an evidence-based teacher!
- If no, think of one area of the topic which you know your students will struggle with and plan which **one** extra sensory method you will use.
- Collect or develop the resources you need.

Quiz to check understanding

True or false. *(Answers on p. 158)*

1. Students have different 'Learning Styles'. You need to use the different senses to allow all students to learn.
2. You create stronger memories if it contains more than one sensory component.
3. We all have both visual and auditory Working Memory, so it makes sense to make use of both types.

FURTHER READING

Ceri Dean. (2012) *Classroom Instruction that Works.* Ch 5: Non-linguistic representations.

Institute for Educational Sciences. (2007) *Organizing Instruction and Study to Improve Student Learning.* Recommendation 3: Combine graphics with verbal descriptions.

Sherrington and Caviglioli. (2020) *Teaching WalkThrus.* P 70: Dual coding.

METHOD 4: ADVANCE ORGANISERS

Overview

An Advance Organiser is a way to communicate what the whole topic will be about to your students. Often in visual/graphical form, it shows the main content in ways the student will easily understand.

Case study

Mr F teaches Carpentry and Joinery at an FE college. During their first year, the students have to learn how to select, measure and cut wood, use hand and machine tools and use fixings and finishes. Part way through that year Mr F has noticed that quite a few students who were enthusiastic at the start of the course become disengaged. He questions several of them. They tell him that they came on the course to be able to fit windows and doors, etc. to buildings, but they don't seem anywhere near doing that.

Later we will see how Mr F solved this with an Advance Organiser.

Refer back to the Advance Organiser from time to time as you go through the topic to remind them how this part of the detail fits into the big picture.

About Advance Organisers

To make the topic more accessible you first divide it into about five sections. You then create your Advance Organiser, presenting the five sections in a graphical way to your students. As you go through the topic you can add to the Advance Organiser and develop it into a graphic for the topic with more detail.

The topic is elephants and you have worked out that it will cover trunks, ears, legs, feeding and communications. One approach is to use a table like the one below.

Elephants	
Trunks	
Ears	
Legs	
Feeding	
Communication	

FIGURE 5.9

At first the column on the right is blank, but you will fill it in as the topic progresses. You may say to the class: 'We're going to be learning about elephants, and it's going to cover trunks and ears, and legs, feeding and communication. We're starting with "trunks" today'. You teach about trunks and they do the activity about trunks etc.

Next lesson you show them the Advance Organiser again. You may say something like: 'Remember the topic is about elephants and yesterday we learned about trunks'. You may well do a quick quiz or ask questions to check their learning. (See later section of 'Questioning as feedback'.) You then start to add some key ideas to the right-hand column. Perhaps about its length and uses – 'used to pull grass and leaves, for drinking and breathing'.

A more common method is to use a mind-map like the one below.

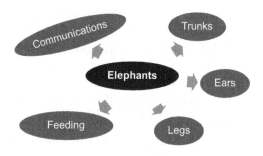

FIGURE 5.10

You may present the Advance Organiser in the same way as the one above. Perhaps the students draw it in the middle of a large sheet of paper and build it up as the topic progresses, into a mind-map of the whole topic.

However, it is vital to keep in mind that the main purpose of the Advance Organiser is to help the student see where the current detail fits into the bigger picture.

Case study: FE Carpentry and Joinery

Mr F teaches Carpentry and Joinery at an Further Education (FE) college. During their first year the students have to learn how to select, measure and cut wood, how to cut joints, how to use hand and machine tools, about glues, screws and other fixings and about finishing with paint, varnish, etc. Part way through that year Mr F has noticed that quite a few students who were enthusiastic at the start of the course become disengaged. He questions several of them – who tell him that they came on the course to be able to fit windows and doors, etc. to buildings, but they don't seem anywhere near doing that.

Mr F creates an Advance Organiser. At the centre is a picture of a door with the label 'Hanging a door'. Around it he has other pictures with labels such as 'measuring', 'cutting', 'joints', 'fixings' and 'finishes'.

At the beginning of the course he explains that these are all the skills needed to fit a real door in a real house. As the course progresses, he refers back to the Advance Organiser to remind the students why they are learning this section.

Case study: Sociology degree

Ms P is teaching Sociology at university. The unit covers 12 sessions. She creates an Advance Organiser mind-map with the main subdivisions: Family, Race, Gender, Social class, Language, Religion.

She uploads the mind-map to the online course area and refers back to it as the course progresses.

Do it collaboratively

Advance Organisers (AOs) are one of the simplest ways to improve learning; however, it is not easy to create a good one. A good plan is to store the Advance Organisers centrally with your scheme of work so that individual teachers do not have to 'reinvent the wheel'. Once you have created and tested one with your topic, add it to the Scheme of Work.

Keep it simple

Case study

Ms P teaches A-level. She has made a slide which is six jigsaw pieces joined together. She labels each piece with part of the course and colours them all red.

As she covers the material in her lessons she changes the colour of the piece to amber when they have covered it in lessons and the students have shown some aptitude. Later, when her assessments show near mastery, she turns the piece to green. Her aim is for the whole Advance Organiser to be green by the end of the topic.

Take care with how often you show the Advance Organiser to the class. If you see them every day, perhaps every lesson is too much.

Case study

Mr J has attended a training session on evidence-based teaching and enthusiastically creates an Advance Organiser for his A-level Physics class. Thinking he needed to do this, each day he shows the class the Advance Organiser. Soon the class are bored with it. 'Why do you show this to us every day?' they ask. Mr J shares the problem with his colleagues. They realise that using the Advance Organiser every time you see the students is probably appropriate at GCSE level, when they only see the students two lessons a week, but at A-level the Advance Organiser is only needed every now and then as the topic develops.

Use non-technical language

It's important that the Advance Organiser communicates the information immediately and only in language that the students already know. It shouldn't contain technical language that they haven't learnt yet.

For example, let's say the topic includes 'photosynthesis'. You may be tempted to use that word in your Advance Organiser on the basis that the students will be learning what it is soon and the Advance Organiser will make sense. However, the main aim of the Advance Organiser is convey a message right at the start, so it is better to use the answer you might give to the student who asks: 'What's photosynthesis?' You may answer: 'How plants make food'. Go with that short statement on the Advance Organiser.

It's important to follow the guidelines for an Advance Organiser as this case study illustrates.

Case study: FE College Sport

Ms C is running a training session with tutors at an FE college. The teachers are sitting in department groups. She explains Advance Organisers and tasks the teachers with creating one for their chosen topic. Most tables are active, but one shows no activity.

Ms C asks the group: 'Do you not think this is appropriate for your subject?' She gets this reply: 'Yes, but we do it already'. Curious, she asks what they do. 'We give every student a photocopy of the course specification at the start of the year'.

They have missed the point. This long, detailed document, which probably includes technical language the students do not yet know, is also far too detailed to be an Advance Organiser.

Why this method works

The brain processes information in two different ways – the 'big picture' and the detail. As the teacher we have both parts clear in our minds. When we start to teach the topic, we are assuming that, as the student gains the detail knowledge we are imparting, that they will also build up the big picture of what it means. This assumption can be a mistake.

Students' skills are not uniform. Some are better at the 'detail' and can use it to build the big picture. They tend to be those who are also good at reading because written material is organised like this. The good reader starts reading the storybook (or topic material) and, as one word leads to the next, the big picture develops in their minds.

Other students are not so good at this route. Many of those who struggle with reading are better at the big picture. As adults, they may become entrepreneurs, architects, builders, garden designers, etc. – they start with a big picture plan and only later fill in the detail.

Advance Organisers start with the big picture. This has positive effects for those who think that way, but does not disadvantage those who process detail more effectively.

The reason for limiting the number of sub-divisions to five or six is because this is the Working Memory Limit. The reason for using only words they understand is the need to link to Prior Knowledge.

When should I use this method in my classroom?

The short answer is: with every course and topic. Although the introduction to this book we suggest that you should not try more than two new things at once, using an Advance Organiser is almost risk-free and is unlikely to go wrong. Sure you will get better and quicker at making them, but even poor-quality Advance Organisers are better than none.

You can make Advance Organisers at different levels:

- For the whole three-year degree course
- For the material you will cover this year
- For the topic you are covering now.

Putting this method into action

- Pick a topic you will be teaching soon.
- Make a list of the main concepts or sub-divisions in the topic material.

- Reduce the number to five or six by combining them to focus on the main messages.
- Create your draft Advance Organiser (AO), trying to use only words you are confident they know the meaning of.
- Show the Advance Organiser to your students and ask them to tell you any words they do not understand.
- Revise your Advance Organiser using the feedback.
- Use it with you class at the beginning of the topic: 'In this unit we are going to be learning about…'.
- Refer back to the Advance Organiser at regular intervals. If you see these students only once a week, use the Advance Organiser every time. If you see them every day, use the Advance Organiser as you move onto the next section.
- Share your Advance Organiser with colleagues and discuss different options at staff meetings.
- Add the improved Advance Organiser to your scheme of work for other teachers to share.

Alternative types of Advance Organiser

The purpose of the Advance Organiser is to tell the students what the course will cover, so anything that does that will be effective.

Story as Advance Organiser

One suggestion is to use a story which covers the topic. It seems that the brain has evolved to understand and retain stories very well (compared to more logical lists, etc.). A geography topic about mountains could be introduced using a story about someone making a journey through the environment. A history topic about a war could use the story of one person's experience.

Skim reading as Advance Organiser

With students with good literacy skills, skim reading the textbook can also provide an overview. Ask the students to read only the headlines (or just the first sentence of each paragraph) and to look at any illustrations.

Quiz to check understanding

True or false. *(Answers on p. 158)*

1. Students store knowledge in two levels – the detail and the big picture. An Advance Organiser gives students the big picture first.
2. You should not use Advance Organisers with good readers as it inhibits their learning.
3. It is important to create your Advance Organiser exactly as described here, otherwise it will not be effective.

FURTHER READING

Ceri Dean. (2012) *Classroom Instruction that Works*. Ch 4: Cues, Questions and Advance Organisers.

Sherrington and Caviglioli. (2020) *Teaching WalkThrus*. P74: Big picture, Small picture.

Note: In an internet search, also use 'Advance Organizer' (the American spelling).

METHOD 5: LINKING ABSTRACT IDEAS TO CONCRETE ANALOGIES

Overview

This is a special case of 'Linking to Prior Knowledge' seen earlier in this chapter. We have given it a separate section partly because it appears separately in the evidence lists we have used, partly because it needs its own explanation and partly because, while everyone needs to implement 'linking to prior knowledge', you will only need to implement this method when dealing with abstract ideas.

We explain what abstract ideas are and compare them with concrete ideas. We explain why some students find them difficult and then show how similes, analogies and metaphors can be used to link these difficult concepts with things the student already knows.

What is an 'abstract' idea?

An Abstract Idea is one that cannot be directly experienced through the senses. They contrast with 'concrete' ideas which can be so experienced. They are the parts of the course which lower-achieving students find most difficult and which are often needed to achieve high grades.

Example: When learning about plants, most students are able to grasp the concrete idea *'plants need water to grow'* either because they have experienced that directly ('I forgot to water the flower-pot and the plant went limp and died', or they can experience it as a demonstration in the classroom. It is factual knowledge which does not require an explanation to grasp it. However, students find it much harder to understand the diffusion of water into roots or the osmosis which keeps the leaves from going limp.

However, it is important not to get too 'hung up' on the definition as it is more of a spectrum that a binary either/or.

Identifying what is abstract

We can identify them in a number of ways:

1. Can you experience it directly with the senses?
2. Ask 'What are the parts of the course that your more able students find relatively easy, but which the lower achieving struggle with and sometimes never get?'
3. Look at the question type. Questions which start with What? Where? How many? or When? are factual recall, descriptive, concrete questions. (Note the most Mastermind and University Challenge questions are of this type!)

However, questions which require some thinking process are abstract. They start with words like Why?, How? or What if? They are always harder.

For example: If you are teaching students about Napoleon's invasion of Russia, concrete questions could be 'When did he invade?', 'How many troops?' while abstract questions could be 'Why did he invade?' or 'What might have happened if Napoleon had waited till Spring?'

Table 5.1 gives some examples to illustrate the difference between concrete and abstract ideas.

Table 5.1

Concrete	Abstract
Table, car, TV, sister, hot, tomorrow, foot	Success, freedom, socialism, democracy, radiation, intension
Heavy things sink	It sinks if its density is greater than the density of the liquid
You breathe in oxygen and breathe out carbon dioxide	Gas exchange takes place between the air in the alveoli and the blood
Plants get water through their roots	Water diffuses through the cell membrane of the root hair cells
Weather map with sun and cloud symbols	Weather maps with isobars and weather fronts
The 'flow' of water over your hands	The 'flow' of money in the economy
The building itself	An architects drawing of the building

Examples of Abstract Ideas

We have done this with a group of teachers of different subjects. These are some of the responses:

- Suggesting an alternative ending for a story
- Identifying intention in a character
- Designing or planning something
- Evaluating their own work (or someone else's)
- Interpreting graphs
- Scales and ratios, proportion, percentage
- Ratios of variables: pressure, concentration, acceleration, density
- Diffusion, osmosis, chemical reactions
- Using theories

- Using symbols
- In art, estimating the result of mixing two colours of paint.

Case study

It's the first lesson after lunch. Two boys are eating their sandwiches in the classroom. They both know this is wrong.

The teacher challenges one. 'James! What DO you think you're doing!?' James looks sheepish, 'Oh, sorry, Sir'. He puts the sandwich away.

The teacher challenges the other one. 'Alex! What DO you think you're doing!?' Alex looks disdainful. 'Eating a sandwich! What does it look like!?' He carries on eating.

James was able to process the implied meaning of the teacher's question. Alex used concrete thinking to understand only the literal meaning if the words.

Alex will struggle with the more abstract concepts in all of his lessons.

Why are Abstract Ideas so hard?

If we look back to the way memories are formed in the brain, we can see a problem for abstract memories – there is nothing to link to! In other words, it is impossible for us humans to form memories of Abstract Ideas themselves.

We all learn about Abstract Ideas by linking them to concrete examples. Your 'more able' students do this automatically and give the impression that they can form abstract memories. Lower-achieving students find this more difficult and need much more help. We need to make (and repeat) the link explicitly.

This means that the only way to understand and remember an Abstract Idea is via link to a concrete idea which is already familiar to the student.

Case study: University Philosophy

Mr B is trying to teach the abstract Buddhist concepts of 'anatman', which is often translated as 'No-self'. Students often struggle and misunderstand the concept, believing that there is no self.

Mr B gives the concrete example of a plant growing in some soil. He first asks what the plant needs to stay alive. Students readily offer 'sun', 'water', minerals', etc. He asks if the plant can exist without these things. Students are clear that it cannot. Mr B explains that, since the plant cannot exist separately from these things, it has no separate existence – and this is 'anatman'.

Applying the method

Linking using similes and analogies

If we look again at the Marzano/Dean list in Chapter 1 we see 'Similes and Analogies' come top of their list of effective methods. They do not appear as a separate section in our combined list because they are an example of ways to connect new learning to prior knowledge.

These are methods which show the learner either what something is like, or not-like and comes in several types:

Simile: saying that object A is like object B and usually includes the word 'like' or 'as'. Examples: "as green as grass"; "...like an old woman"; "diesel is like petrol, but thicker". Sometimes there are also differences stated. "backstroke is like front crawl, but on your back"; "a bolt is like a screw, it has a thread and you turn it, but the thread goes into a nut, not wood".

Analogy: saying that process A is like process B. Examples: "he was running around like a headless chicken". "Trying to get Jim to do his homework is like trying to get the cat into a box – it keeps jumping out".

Metaphor: same structure as an analogy, but without the word "like". Examples: "her smile was the morning Sun"; "my teenage son has turned into a gorilla"; "a battle of ideas".

Allegory, Fable: a story which is a metaphor. Examples: books like Animal Farm, Pilgrim's Progress, and Aesop's Fables.

Parable: An allegory which gives a moral message: (e.g. New Testament Bible stories)

It is essential that the thing you are saying it is 'like' must be familiar to the learner. There is little point in creating analogies to things which the student does not already know. A common fault is to believe that, if you can give real-life examples of what you are trying to teach, then learning will be improved. However, if the example is also not known to the student they now have three things to learn, not one: the example, the idea you are teaching PLUS the way they are linked!

Here is an example of a teacher making a concrete link when the students are struggling.

Case study: Yr 4 'Earth and Space'

Ms K is teaching about the Moon to her Yr 4 class. She notices that some students think that the Moon is a source of light. She tries to explain that it is a reflection, and is not shining, but the students are struggling.

She uses a concrete example: shining a torch onto a mirror and a white piece of cloth to demonstrate that they can see things by reflection as the cloth is clearly not shining.

Why this method works

We have seen a version of Figure 5.11 before. It shows how the concept 'Pope' is understood by its links to more familiar things like king and father. However, we can also see that there is something in common between the relationship between the Pope and the church, a king and his country and a father and his family – they are all 'heads of...' something.

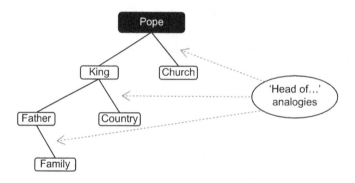

FIGURE 5.11

Without us being aware of it, our brain organises memories with these analogous links. We can see that this happens automatically if we look at some simply analogy questions:

■ Head is to hat as hand is to ????
■ Cup is to drink as plate is to ????

The answers to these riddles pop into our heads without us having to think very hard. The brain seems to have stored the links between the *'where clothes fit'* and *'which crockery to use'* answers without us having decided to do so!

The diagram shows that:

- The father is head of a family.
- A king is head of a country.
- The Pope is head of the Catholic Church.

This means we have a powerful learning tool available to us when teaching our students. They will easily find the links if we offer an analogy and then use the automatic analogy links as a way to connect the new idea to something already known – even if it is a quite different subject.

For example: In Business Studies we can use the same analogy link to explain the relationship between the Chief Executive (CEO) and the rest of the organisation.

Although many Abstract Ideas are introduced only at GCSE level, they occur at any age.

Case Study: Yr 2 Maths

Ms K finds that the best way to help her students with a new maths concept is to do it in three stages. First with concrete objects, such as paper cups or blocks, then pictorially, with the shapes on the board and only with the abstract symbols ('3', '+' or '%' etc.).

Case Study: Yr 6 Writing

Mr F finds that his students find the concept of 'cohesion' difficult to grasp. He uses the analogy of a flowing river. He finds that cohesion can be shown by acting out the story they have written. One student's story has a character in one paragraph in the living room and in the next he is in the kitchen, with no process of how he got there. The acting-out shows the jump, or lack of cohesion.

Once the concept is grasped through examples, the word 'cohesion' can be used and understood. Without the concrete example links it would have been difficult for most of his students.

When should I use this method in my classroom?

When first starting to apply the effective methods in this book, this is not necessarily one you use straight away. Methods should only be used when you have identified a learning need.

Let's say you notice that many of your students are struggling with one part of your topic. The first thing is to check that the problem is not something simple such as missing prior knowledge.

You can spot when the problem is connected with something abstract by asking the questions which identify something as abstract:

- Can it be experienced with the senses, or does it require a thinking process?
- Is it a factual question: When? Where? or How many?, or one requiring thinking: How? Why? What if…?
- Are your lower-achieving students struggling with this concept while the higher-achievers are doing fine?

Putting this method into action

First identify the abstract content in your topic using the criteria above.

Pick some of the keywords from a topic you will be teaching. Find similes to explain them. (Make sure you are linking to something your students already know.)

Now find a process (colouring hair; using a chainsaw; writing a CV…) and come up with an analogy for that. Sometimes this is a longer story which paints a picture in the mind of the learner.

Quiz to check understanding

True or false. *(Answers on p. 159)*

1. Quiz programmes like *Mastermind* test abstract thinking.
2. Abstract Ideas cannot be directly experienced with the senses.
3. Linking an Abstract Idea to a concrete example is helpful, but not vital.

FURTHER READING

Institute for Educational Sciences. (2007) *Organizing Instruction and Study to Improve Student Learning*. Recommendation 4: Connect and integrate abstract and concrete representations of concepts.

Geoff Petty. (2018) *Teach Even Better*. Ch2: Teaching the hard stuff.

Sherrington and Caviglioli. (2020) *Teaching WalkThrus*. P76: Abstract models with concrete examples.

6

Setting challenging tasks

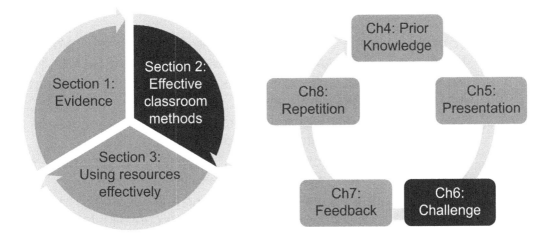

In Chapter 5, we looked at effective ways to present new information to students. This chapter looks at effective ways to set tasks for your students to apply and develop their new knowledge.

WHAT IS 'CHALLENGE'?

The chapter title is 'Setting challenging tasks' because of the central role of 'challenge' to learning.

There are two ways to set a task which will result in no new learning:

- The task you set is too easy: your students are only exercising their current knowledge.
- The task is too hard: most students cannot do it.

Although not often addressed, 'setting a challenging task' is something nearly all teachers do subconsciously as they develop their expertise. Most of us have had the experience of setting tasks which are too hard, particularly when we started teaching. It is also a common feature of lessons taught by politicians and journalists who come to a school and teach a few lessons.

A 'challenging task' is one where your students succeed with a bit of struggle. They may need to consult the textbook, ask you (or their neighbour) a question, discuss the task in a group, attempt it and get feedback etc.

IN THIS CHAPTER

We set out five ways to make the tasks you set more effective for learning:

1. To know what the task is, you can use **Modelling and Worked Examples** to show what a good answer or product would look like.
2. You can set tasks which are not just words by setting **Graphical and other Non-linguistic** tasks.
3. You can get your students to improve their planning, monitoring and evaluation using **Metacognition**.
4. If students work effectively in groups, **Cooperative or Collaborative methods** are effective to promote thinking.
5. **Thinking tasks**, such as problem solving and hypothesis testing, can deepen your students' knowledge and consolidate the surface thinking.

FURTHER READING

Allison and Tharby. (2015) *Making Every Lesson Count.* Ch 1: Challenge.

METHOD 1: MODELLING AND WORKED EXAMPLES

Overview

Before a student can create a good piece of work they need to know what 'good' looks like. In practical subjects it is common for the trainer to demonstrate (model) the skill to the learner and then to provide feedback during the learning process, again with physical demonstrations.

This method involves extending this approach into the classroom in all subjects.

Case study: Yr 8 Maths

Ms L, a Geography teacher, is covering a Yr 8 Maths class for an absent colleague. She looks at the work set and realises she is moderately familiar with the maths. She glances in the textbook provided and works through two examples on the whiteboard and then sets the cover work.

As she circulates, one student says 'Can you be our Maths teacher? You're way better than ours'. At first Ms L first gets a rush of pride, but then asks the students for their reasons. 'You leave the examples up on the board; our regular teacher always rubs them off'.

About Modelling and Worked Examples

Modelling and Worked Examples involve showing the students what the final result should look like and the process by which you achieved it.

■ Multiplication. Several Worked Examples of the method demonstrated on the board can be left visible when you set different calculations for the students.
■ Essay writing. Examples for poor, good and excellent work can be shown together with a discussion of why they are good, poor, etc. (best not to use your students' work for this).
■ PE. The exact task is demonstrated, students need to reproduce it.

As 'Modelling' is one of their six principles, Allison and Tharby have a whole chapter on this. They suggest there are numerous ways to do modelling:

■ 'Live' modelling: you show the process in front of your students.
■ 'Prepare in advance' modelling: you prepare the model beforehand and show the students.

■ 'Admire each other' modelling: you show the rest of the class a good piece of work by one student or get students to circulate and see what others have done.

(Allison and Tharby 2015)

Other types of Worked Example

It is not always necessary to give the students a version of a good answer. You could also give them versions of weak and average answers for them to see the difference. You can also use a discursive method to get the students to identify pitfalls and misconceptions and develop a 'good answer' using class questioning.

What is important is not so much which modelling method you use, it is whether the student has a clear idea of what a 'good answer' is, and how to achieve it, before they can do one themselves.

Case study: Secondary English
Mr P is teaching a story in a secondary English class. He has set the task (a typical exam question) for them to make notes about five characters in the story. When he marks them, some are good, but one misses out a character and another covers one character in just one sentence.

The next time Mr P teaches this skill, he shows his class three examples from the previous class's work (names erased!) and discusses the three answers with his class. He finds that, when assessing the other students' work, the students give similar marks to those the examiner might give.

Later Mr P sets the same task with characters from a different text. The results are a significant improvement.

The following is a variant which can be used if you feel that simply giving the students a ready-made Worked Example is not appropriate. (Graphical Organisers are explained in the next method in this chapter.)

Case study: Graphical Organisers. Co-created Worked Example
Ms K is training her class to use Graphical Organisers (GOs). After briefly explaining the idea to the class she gets them to draft a GO themselves. Students then compare their draft with a partner and each makes suggestions for improvement, giving their reasoning.

Ms K circulates, offering prompts and asking questions. Occasionally, she stops the class to discuss a particular point. The Worked Example is co-created by this process. As the students are actively involved in the process, more learning has taken place than if a ready-made version was given.

Interleaving Worked Examples

One approach is to alternate (interleave) Worked Examples and problems for your students. Research shows that, in subjects like Maths and Science, this approach is far more effective than simply setting the tasks (even though the students will only do half the number of calculations) and quite a lot better than showing all the worked examples at the start.

In some ways this process is similar to the feedback effects show in a later chapter. The student is given repeated opportunities to think about the knowledge that they need to use. This means they are less likely to practice a mistaken technique.

Why this method works

In the previous chapter we looked at Working Memory capacity and the concept of Cognitive Load. Using a Worked Example is a way to reduce cognitive load by setting out the steps needed to succeed. To achieve a task we not only need the knowledge, we also need the framework for presenting the knowledge – whether it's an essay, furniture making, maths problem or labelled map.

When learning a practical task, we need to set up pathways (memories) in our brain which store the actions needed, for instance, to serve a tennis ball. By seeing someone else serve, we can start to learn what the process involves. The same is true in non-practical tasks such as writing a story. If we have seen the process of someone else creating a story, have seen the steps involved and what a good story looks like, we can learn the task much more easily.

After some practice and suitable feedback we do develop a sense of what is needed. For example, publicity people get a feel for what a good advertisement looks like; journalists know how to write an effective article, etc.

When should I use this method in my classroom?

This should be your regular practice. Whether you are asking your students to paint a picture, write a story, cut some hair, design an experiment, make some furniture, do a calculation or analyse a poem, they all need to know what the task involves.

There is a link here to the Advance Organiser in the previous chapter: you are showing the student what the big picture or final product will look like.

Notice, however, the degree to which you already do this as it is often part of your normal teaching practice. Having read this method, make an assessment of your own practice to judge how well you are already doing.

One indicator that a Worked Example is needed is when your student has made no progress and, when challenged, says something like: 'I don't know where to start'. The Worked Example shows the process and so, how to start.

Case study: Yr 1 talk partners

Ms T often uses 'talk partners' in her lessons. She gets her students to discuss something in pairs and then questions the students. However, she has found from experience that many of her students have no idea how to have such a conversation! She models the discussion with her Classroom Assistant, sometimes doing it badly and asking her students what was wrong.

Putting this method into action

- Identify a learning task, particularly one where students have struggled in the past.
- Create a model piece of work (perhaps on a parallel topic) and show the students what it is like to be 'good'.
- Possible: prepare two other pieces of work which you would rate as 'poor' and 'excellent' and make these available.
- When the students have done their piece of work, get them to revisit the exemplars and assess themselves.

Quiz to check understanding

True or false? *(Answers on p. 159)*

1. Most students can understand the task if it is explained well.
2. Worked Examples show what the final product should be like.
3. The best Worked Examples are generated by the teacher.

REFERENCE LIST AND FURTHER READING

Allison and Tharby. (2015) *Making Every Lesson Count*. Ch 3: 'Modelling'.

Institute for Educational Sciences. (2007) *Organizing Instruction and Study to Improve Student Learning*. Recommendation 2: Interleave worked example solutions and problem-solving exercises.

Geoff Petty. (2018) *Teach Even Better*. Ch 7: Modelling.

Barak Rosenshine. (2012) *Principles of Instruction*. Principle 4: Provide models.

METHOD 2: GRAPHICAL AND NON-LINGUISTIC METHODS

Prior Knowledge quiz

True or false? *(Answers on p. 156)*

1. Long-term memories are stored in the brain as connections between neurons.
2. 'Dual coding' involves explaining the new concept in two different ways.
3. When you first try a new method in the classroom it may not work well.

Overview

As we saw in the last chapter, we can use non-linguistic methods, such as graphics or animation, to present new material. We can use the same methods when we set a challenging task.

> ### Case study: University Education degree
> Mr N often asks his students to read a chapter in preparation for the next topic. Many students fail to do the task.
>
> He changes his approach. Now he asks them to read the chapter (on '*Theories of Intelligence*') and make a mind map of the main ideas which they must bring to the next lesson. He finds that a much higher percentage attempt this task.

Graphical Organisers

This method involves getting your students to arrange the material in a graphical format.

Graphical Organisers (GOs) consist of words in boxes, connected or arranged in different ways. We can use Graphical Organisers to help

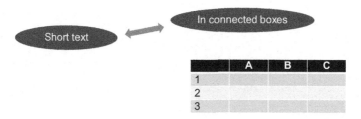

FIGURE 6.1

students organise their knowledge. By arranging the information visually, we not only get the benefits of dual coding, but also sort the information in ways similar to those used by the brain to store the knowledge.

Applying the method

This is not a 'quick and easy' method as you will need to become familiar with using the different GOs yourself and then train your students to use them. The general advice for developing the skill of using these effective methods is not to try too much at once and allow yourself time to develop the skills.

When we use Graphic Organisers (GO) to present information to our students (see Multi-sensory approach) we help them see the relationships as a set of connections. Using a GO in your presentation has a positive effect on learning, but having your students create their own GOs has an even higher effect.

There are three main types of GO: those which describe or define something; those which compare; and those which show a sequence of cause.

GOs which define or describe

In the examples below we see several options.

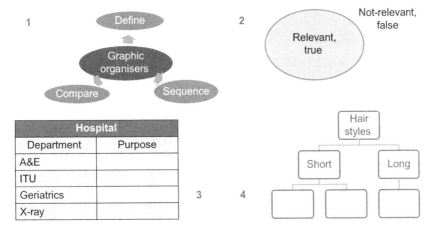

FIGURE 6.2

1. Shows different types of Graphic Organisers.
2. Used to sort the relevant from the non-relevant, e.g. causes of inflation.

3.   Define roles, e.g. of departments in a hospital.
4.   Defining different hairstyles.

GOs which compare

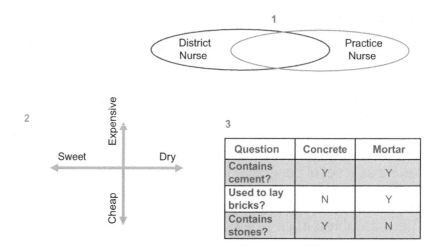

FIGURE 6.3

1.   Comparing the role of a District Nurse with a Practice Nurse, with a section in the middle showing what all nurses do.
2.   Comparing wines on two scales: sweet/dry and on cost.
3.   Comparing concrete and mortar. (Useful for similar concepts which your students often get muddled.)

GOs which show a sequence or cause

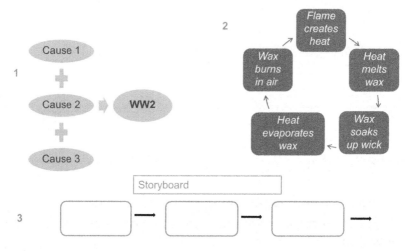

FIGURE 6.4

1. Showing multiple causes of one effect, e.g. causes of the Second World War.
2. Showing a cycle of effects, e.g. a candle burning.
3. Putting something in chronological order, e.g. a storyboard or timeline.

Case study: 6th form English

Ms M is studying a play with her 6th form English class. She wants them to compare the internal and external influences on the characters. Instead of simply making a list, she gets the groups to draw round one member to create an outline on a roll of paper and then write in internal influences (e.g. love and anxiety) inside the outline and external factors (e.g. parental expectations and events) outside.

Ms M realises that because the exercise was hands-on, discursive and visual they are much more likely to recall it later.

We met Mr N and his undergraduates at the beginning of this method. This is how he developed his method.

Case study: University Education degree

Mr N often asks his students to read a chapter in preparation for the next topic. Many students fail to do the task.

He changes his approach. Now he asks them to read the chapter (on 'Theories of Intelligence') and make a mind-map of the main ideas which they must bring to the next lesson. He finds that a much higher percentage attempt this task.

He then uses a variation of 'think, pair, share' and first gets students to compare their mind-map with their neighbour's and then leads a class discussion using students' work. Students develop their own mind-map during the discussion.

The graphic provides the focus for the conversation between the students and between the students and the teacher.

This combines the use of graphical methods with 'summarising': finding the main points in the topic.

Why this method works

Firstly, as we saw in Section 1, memories in the brain are networks of connections between the component parts. However, when we teach using spoken or written words, we deliver the material as a linear flow.

The student has to work out the relationship between these parts for themselves. When presented visually, the relationship between the parts and the whole are immediately apparent.

Secondly, GOs are a form of dual coding, using both the visual and verbal pathways in the brain. As we have seen before, the more connections we link, the stronger the memory.

Thirdly, when students are working on a graphic (rather than text) the graphic becomes the focus of discussion either with other students or between teacher and student. It is so much easier to discuss something if you are pointing to and looking at the same thing.

When should I use this method in my classroom?

GOs are a very effective way to improve learning, especially if you use them rarely at the moment. However, you should not jump in too quickly. There are, as you see above, many different GOs to choose from.

This is not a method to use without practice, both by yourself and by your students (see below).

Putting this method into action

Becoming familiar

- Decide what type of GO to choose: define/explain, compare or show sequence/cause.
- Choose one format and experiment with its use.
- Introduce the idea of GOs to the class and get them used to the idea off re-arranging material graphically. Initially choose something very simple.

Applying GOs to course material

- Present the new material.
- Students create a suitable GO to summarise the topic, or to answer a specific question.
- Students circulate and look at other organisers for good ideas.
- Students improve their work.
- Peer or self-assessment against criteria you provide.

Other non-linguistic tasks

In the previous chapter we saw the use of non-linguistic methods to present new information to your students. We can set the same sorts of tasks for our students.

Case study: Business Yr 10

Ms P is starting to teach Business, Enterprise and Entrepreneurship at the beginning of Yr 10 to students with no prior knowledge of the subject. She knows from past experience that trying to teach the theoretical material straight away has not worked, so the first term, right through till February, is all practical.

The students are organised in teams and each team is given £50 (real money) which they use to create items for sale on market stalls and school days. Teams are in competition with each other. For example, they have a market stall selling hampers. This means they must first make hampers, then sell them and do the finances using real money.

The project contains many of the topics they will study on their course, including project management, record keeping, etc. The plan is written on a board so both they and Ms P can visually see what needs to be done. They do several such events to cement the practical learning.

Later, in Yr 11, when they are studying finance, she can link to this prior knowledge and say 'Remember when we...'.

Case study: Yr 10 English

Ms D is teaching 'A Christmas Carol' to a lower-achieving group. To help them remember and understand the story she creates a storyline on the wall of the classroom.

She creates a timeline and adds the plot of the story to it. Then she adds images of the characters and other pictures of life in Victorian Britain, workhouses, etc.

As the class progresses through the novel they add to the timeline e.g. linking characters or noting how their sympathy for Scrooge develops throughout.

A more physically active lesson can help students secure long-term memories of what they have learned. One teacher reported how he had done a 'Space' demonstration in an assembly with his students acting as planets, moons, etc. To avoid the possibility that students will be more focussed on their acting than the learning, this needs to be done to secure new learning.

Here is another example:

Case study: Secondary science

Ms H has taught her lower-achieving class about the endocrine system. However, she soon realises that most have not learned it sufficiently.

She creates some roles: pituitary gland, pancreas, liver, insulin, etc. and assigns students to the roles.

She discusses the role with the students and they then create mini-plays where the process is acted out with either the student saying what they are doing, or Ms H runs a commentary.

Ms H does this for a lot of 'systems' and reports that it really helped her students to understand the order of events and role of each part.

Here is another novel idea:

Case study: Spanish language

Ms K is teaching how to give directions in Spanish. Rather than a 'pen and paper' exercise, she gets students to use Google Maps on phone/tablet. She gives them a starting place and destination in Barcelona and gives the task to describe the route between two places.

Students open 'street view' and follow the route. They then need to describe the route – turn right, turn left, straight on, walk 200 m – in Spanish.

If the online facility is not available, Ms K has used a simpler version where students direct one person in their group in a route around the classroom.

Quiz to check understanding

True or false? *(Answers on p. 159)*

1. A 'challenging task' is one which the students find difficult.
2. Using multi-sensory methods confuses the student and makes learning slower.
3. So long as you are well planned, it is safe to try out a new teaching method for a whole lesson.

REFERENCE LIST AND FURTHER READING

Oliver Caviglioli. (2019) *Dual Coding for Teachers* John Catt.

Ceri Dean. (2012) *Classroom Instruction That Works*. Ch 5: Non-linguistic representations.

Geoff Petty. (2018) *Teach Even Better*. p 45: Graphic Organisers.

METHOD 3: METACOGNITION

Overview

The word 'metacognition' sounds a bit complicated and theoretical, and so does not sound the sort of thing you might find useful in the classroom. However, when we see the practical applications we can see that we already use metacognitive strategies in our classrooms. Whenever we ask 'What is your plan?' or 'How is it going?' or 'What will you do to start?', you are asking metacognitive questions which clarify your students' thinking.

'Cognition' means 'thinking'. 'Metacognition' means 'thinking about your thinking'.

Teaching metacognition involves getting your students to reflect on their own learning by actively talking about how they will plan something, how well they are progressing and finally how well they did.

In this case study we see that the student initially misinterprets the question. It takes practice for your students to realise that they need to describe their thinking process, not just give the answer.

Case study: Yr 2 Maths

Mr A is teaching Maths to Yr 2. He asks 'How would you add 32 + 24?' One student answers '56'. Mr A explains that he doesn't want the answer, he wants them to explain how they worked it out. This time, as the student explains the process, Mr A writes on the board to demonstrate the method.

The evidence shows that students who do well at metacognition also do better in their learning and results.

Applying the method

There is a great deal written about metacognition, some of which makes it sound very complicated. This description provides a basic introduction.

We need to get our students thinking about their thinking process by asking them (or getting them to ask themselves) questions while carrying out a task. The task can be broken down into three main stages:

- Planning (before you start)
- Monitoring (while doing the task)
- Evaluating (after the task is finished).

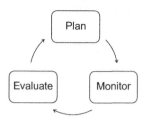

FIGURE 6.5

Planning questions

- What am I trying to achieve? (or learn?)
- What shall I do first?
- What are the steps or parts?
- How much time do I have?
- Have I done something like this before?
- What does a 'good answer' look like?

Monitoring questions

- How am I doing?
- Who could I ask for help?
- What could I do differently?

Evaluation questions

(Note: Students find evaluation much harder than planning and monitoring as they have to see what they have done, as though they were an observer. This is an abstract task.)

- What worked well?
- Can I explain to others how I did this?
- What could I have done better?
- Can I use this approach for other tasks?

Why this method works

There are a number of stages at which students stumble in their learning. They sometimes don't know how to start, they may get stuck with the first idea they had and not look at other options, they may not notice when their plan is not working out, they may be too rigid to change direction and, when they have completed the task, they may not be able to assess how effective their strategy was and simply use the same, mediocre strategy next time.

Metacognition is a way to improve these skills in your student. These are general life skills, equally applicable to gardening, cooking for a group, planning a holiday, etc.

When should I use this method in my classroom?

One of the good things about metacognition is that even a little bit is beneficial. There is a massive complexity in some educational literature which may give the impression that you need a degree in metacognition before you can master it.

However, if we simply start using some of the standard questions listed above, we are already using the method.

> *Case study*
> Ms R has been teaching for years and has usually used a 'hands-up' form of questioning. She reads about metacognition and decides to try something a bit different.
>
> When a student answers her question, she no longer says 'Yes, well done', she replies with 'Why do you think that?', 'What's the evidence for that?' or 'How did you get to that answer?'

Putting this method into action

Metacognition is not so much a distinct method as part of effective classroom practice.

- Model the process yourself by explaining aloud your own planning, monitoring, etc. thinking.
- Teach your students how to plan, monitor and evaluate their work.
- Promote metacognitive talk in the classroom with probing questions.

However, students may need some help articulating their thoughts.

> *Case study: Yr 6 Maths*
> Ms J wants to promote metacognition in her lesson; however, she finds that some students dry up part way through their explanation.
>
> She realises that, while older students and adults may be hearing what they are about to say in their heads before they speak,

with her younger students the first time they hear what they are about to say is when they actually say it! If they are not clear they may just stop part way through.

To overcome this, she repeats what the student has said back to them which gives them the chance to organise their thoughts. She writes what they have said on the board and lets them clarify it, perhaps using persistent questioning.

Quiz to check understanding

True or false? *(Answers on p. 160)*

1. Metacognition is only relevant for older students.
2. Students with good metacognitive skills achieve higher grades.
3. Metacognitive skills developed in one subject can be used in other subjects and situations.

REFERENCE LIST AND FURTHER READING

Churches et al. (2017) *Neuroscience for Teachers*. Ch 3: Metacognition.
Education Endowment Foundation. Toolkit. Metacognition. (Search EEF education toolkit).
Sherrington and Caviglioli. (2020) *Teaching WalkThrus*. p 82: Metacognitive talk.

METHOD 4: COLLABORATIVE METHODS

Overview

The words 'cooperative' and 'collaborative' are used interchangeably and refer to teaching techniques where students do not work on their own, but work together in a group on a shared task.

However, it differs from simply 'working in groups' in that a system is in place which aims to ensure that all team members participate and where the individual (not the group) is assessed for their learning.

Case study

Fred has a problem he is trying to solve, but he doesn't feel he is getting anywhere. He calls his friend Pete and starts to explain the problem to him. Immediately, Fred can see the solution to his own problem. He thanks Pete for his help. Pete replies: 'But, I didn't do anything!'

This case study illustrates the value of working collaboratively: talking about the problem makes the solution easier.

Applying the method

(Note that this method is not the same as 'self-discovery' or 'student-centred' methods where the students are given a topic and, using books, internet, etc., do the learning themselves.)

Working as a pair

The smallest group is a pair. Working in pairs can be great, especially when the task is quite short and setting up teams would be time-consuming.

One option is a questioning strategy. Instead of 'hands up', ask the class to discuss your question in a pair for 30 seconds. Perhaps help them back to quiet with a call of '10 seconds...'. Explain that you will pick on one individual, but that they need to report their discussion, rather than their opinion.

There are distinct advantages to this method:

- Nearly 100% of the students will participate.
- Nearly everyone will have an answer (unlike 'hands-up' questioning).
- Students find it easier to report their discussion as it does not expose them individually.

Think, Pair, Share

This is an extension of the above method. It has three phases:

1. Students think what their answer is alone.
2. They discuss it as a pair.
3. You create a class discussion from the pair-answers.

Choosing the groups

Choose a larger group than two only if it is useful for the task you are setting. Groups should be the size that makes for the most effective discussion. Too small and there may be too few ideas. Too large and not everyone can participate in (or even hear) the discussion.

Sometimes it is useful to choose groups with a range of abilities. If groups contain too many low-achieving students, they may have no ideas at all, or none they are confident to share.

Organising the groups

A common experience of having students working collaboratively is that only some of the group members participate. To overcome this, one option is to give each team member a specific role. There are a number of models for this, here are just two:

Option 1: Group leader, Time keeper, Materials manager, Scribe and Encourager. Team members may be given cards with their 'job description' on the back.

Option 2: TEAMS Talker, Enthusiast, Artist, Manager and Secretary. The Enthusiast provides energy and information, the Artist draws the images, the Secretary write the text, the Manager makes sure everyone is on task and the Talker makes the presentation.

It is important to discuss and model the various roles so that students are familiar with them. For instance, in Option 2, the Talker is the person who will report back on behalf of the group, while the Manager is the person who makes sure everyone participates.

Methods which promote talk and discussion are shown to be the most effective.

Case study

Ms S is revising a topic in the run-up to public exams. She has 30 students in the class and has decided to use the 'TEAMS' approach (Option 2, p. 114). This means there will be five students per team and so six teams in total.

She looks through the topic and divides the content into six sections. She writes the keywords and main ideas on the board and labels which part each group will do.

She has implemented a multi-sensory approach in her teaching and so gives the students a task which is also multi-sensory. They must create a presentation which consists of some visual images (which will be projected using the class visualiser), a verbal narrative which will be spoken as the images are presented and also a kinaesthetic activity to illustrate one aspect of their topic.

Assessment

While the groups work on the same task and sometimes the group task can be assessed, it is also important to assess each pupil individually. If every student knows they will be assessed, they are more likely to participate in the group.

Competition

It is, of course, possible to create some element of competition between groups on the task, but you need to try to ensure that the competition does not become the aim, rather than the learning. If, for example, the groups are creating short presentations as part of a revision process, then you can judge/mark the presentations themselves and perhaps give prizes. However, you will also need to assess the learning of the individuals.

Staff development

Some training in using these methods has been shown to be good value for money (see EEF reference below).

Why this method works

As Fred discovered in the case study at the start of this method, sometimes just 'thinking aloud' is helpful on its own. Notice that his friend does not offer any advice!

In a group there is a higher chance that at least one person will have at least part of the answer or a starting idea. If your student is struggling alone, with a blank mind, they may well simply sit there and not make any progress. The response from another team member to their half-idea, or their response to another team member's idea, significantly increases the chance of good thinking.

On our own we may have ideas which make sense to us, but can easily be pulled apart by others. In a group the ideas can be tested and alternatives considered.

When should I use this method in my classroom?

Using 'discuss in pairs' or 'think, pair share' is low-risk and you can apply them without much practice.

However, if you are not familiar with the larger-group methods you need to 'advance with caution'. If the groups are not organised in a way which means that all team members are engaged, it is common to see one or two group members doing all the work while the others are idly chatting. This negates the value of the technique.

Students also need to be trained to use the method and initially assessed as much for their participation, task completion, etc. as for their learning.

Collaborative methods work best when the basic, surface learning is reasonably secure and the task you are setting is something like thinking skills, problem solving or revising.

Putting this method into action

Once you establish routines etc., this can be a very effective method. However, as with trying all but the simplest new techniques for the first time, make sure you have an alternative lesson if this does not go well first time. Only try it for a short time in a lesson, perhaps towards the end.

1. Create your groups. Usually this is best done by you so that you can choose whether to mix abilities, separate students etc. In some classes it may be fine to let them choose their own groups, but be aware that some individuals may not be chosen by any group and you may have to allocate them to a group.
2. Decide if you are going to use one of the defined-roles methods. If so, introduce them to the students. Perhaps give each group a sheet with the job descriptions.
3. Start with a task which is fairly easy to do. Perhaps they create a Graphical Organiser for the material you have just covered. Perhaps they create some revision materials as in the case study earlier in this method.

4. Circulate and ensure that all students are participating. You may need to prompt individuals, reminding them of their role or question the team to ensure they understand the task.

5. Mark the group effort in some way. They present, you score? They self-assess against criteria? etc.

6. Assess the students individually on their learning (perhaps as part of the topic assessment you planned anyway).

7. Evaluate the experience and make notes for the next attempt. (Remember you will need to try this about three times before you will know whether it's a good method for you, your subject and your students).

Quiz to check understanding

True or false? *(Answers on p. 160)*

1. Working in groups does not work as some students will do nothing towards the task.

2. Collaborative work improves learning by using dialogue to promote thinking.

3. Collaborative tasks work best when you are introducing new material.

REFERENCE LIST AND FURTHER READING

Ceri Dean. (2012) *Classroom Instruction that Works*. Ch 3: Cooperative Learning.

Education Endowment Foundation. Toolkit. Collaborative learning. (Search: EEF Education Toolkit).

Sherrington and Caviglioli. (2020) *Teaching WalkThrus*. p 134: Collaborative Learning.

Dylan Wiliam. (2011) *Embedded Formative Assessment*. Ch 6: Cooperative Learning.

METHOD 5: THINKING TASKS

Prior Knowledge quiz

True or false? *(Answers on p. 156)*

1. New knowledge is connected to Prior Knowledge.
2. If you are well prepared, when you first try a new method in the classroom it will go well.
3. Memories are links to the components of the memory.

Overview

This method contains a range of strategies to take your students from 'surface' to 'deep' thinking. Surface thinking refers to the individual items of factual knowledge etc. Deep thinking involves applying that knowledge in a flexible way.

Case study: Secondary History

Mr R has been teaching about Napoleon's invasion of Russia. He tests the class on their factual knowledge. They score well. They know names, dates and places. He then asks questions like: 'Why did Napoleon invade Russia?', 'What would have happened if Napoleon had waited till spring before attacking?' His students look blankly at him.

Applying the method

The evidence literature includes a number of methods which apply the same general principle:

- Hypothesis testing
- Problem solving
- Concept Cartoons.

Hypothesis testing

A hypothesis is a proposed explanation for something and is the starting point for further investigation. Students grapple with the problem either by designing an experiment to test the hypothesis, or by doing some research to find evidence to test the hypothesis.

We cover this in more detail under 'Putting this method into action' below.

Problem solving

There is an important distinction here between problem-solving teaching, which has an effect-size of 0.6 (high), and problem-based learning, where the effect is 0.15 (very low). The difference is whether the students already have secure, surface knowledge. If you try to get your students to learn the surface knowledge by giving them problems to solve, it is not an effective strategy. However, if the surface knowledge is secure and you set problems to solve (as in 'Hypothesis testing' above), then the technique is very positive.

Concept Cartoons

Concept Cartoons are a visual way to present problems for discussion. The materials consist of a problem and three or four possible solutions (hypotheses). The task is for the students (often in a group) to discuss the options and decide which is the best answer, but also be able to explain their thinking and decision (metacognition).

Case study: Concept Cartoon

Ms W is teaching about heat and insulation. She shows the class a picture of a snowman and a student who is about to put a coat on it. They discuss what effect this will have on the snowman:

Person A thinks the coat will make the snowman melt more quickly. Person B suggests that it will melt more slowly. The coat-holder thinks it will make no difference.

The students discuss which hypothesis is correct, decide on their explanation and then share their answers with the class.

While using a visual like this to give your students options is helpful, it may not always be necessary. You could simply apply this 'multiple option' approach to hypothesis testing.

Case study: Yr 5 History

Mr B is teaching the history of the Vikings in the British Isles. At the end of the unit he gives them a series of questions about the starting with simple 'when', 'where' questions but moving on to more complex questions like 'How would Britain be different if there had been no Vikings?'

The following year he is teaching about the Dunkirk evacuation. With the unit completed and facts learned, he wants them to apply what they had learned. This time his 'Thinking Task' question is 'Was Dunkirk a success or a failure?'

Why this method works

We know that memories in the brain are links. When each piece of information in your topic is being learned, links are being made to the student's prior knowledge, etc. However, the links are not well formed between the items of knowledge. We need to give the students the opportunity to use all the knowledge in a thinking or problem-solving exercise.

In the left-hand diagram of Figure 6.6, the individual pieces of knowledge (white dots and connections) are secure in long-term memory. This student will be able to recall concrete, factual, surface knowledge (e.g. What? Where? When? How many?). It is by engaging with a thinking task that the knowledge is connected as in the right-hand diagram and becomes deep learning.

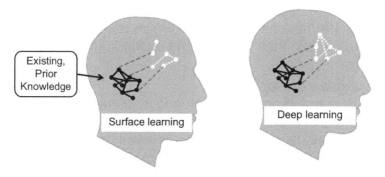

FIGURE 6.6

When should I use this method in my classroom?

This method is best used towards the end of the topic when the basic knowledge is reasonably secure. There is little point in using it too soon as we are trying to make the links between the surface knowledge and, if it is not present, it cannot be linked.

Here is an example of a teacher using 'problem solving' too early and realising the need to change.

Case study: Yr 3 Maths
Ms M is teaching fractions to Yr 3. She starts with simple problems, for example: *a quarter of 12 (using blocks)*.

Once they have grasped the idea she sets them some problems to solve which use fractions. Example: *Mike spends ¼ of his £12 on toys. How much does he have left?* She notices that they are making a lot of mistakes and discovers that the knowledge of fractions is not secure enough.

She gives the students more practice with simple fraction problems, first with blocks, then with play-money and finally on paper, before going on to the problem solving.

Putting this method into action

Hypothesis testing

Think of a question which would require your students to apply their new knowledge. It needs to be one they don't know the answer to and which is not simple, factual knowledge. Here are some examples of hypotheses to test:

- Car mechanics: I think it's the switch, not the bulb.
- Physics: Increasing the weight of the pendulum decreases the weight of the swing.
- Hairdressing: Shorter grey hair makes you look younger.

You could also start with a question that needs a hypothesis. For example:

- Modern history: Why did we invade Iraq?
- Building: Why don't we have the bedrooms downstairs?
- Sociology: Why do men and women wear different clothes?

Students then come up with a hypothesis to test.
Another alternative is to use 'What if…?' questions. For example:

- Building: What if bedrooms were on the ground floor?
- Gardening: What if you took hardwood cuttings in the summer?
- Politics: What if we increased the minimum wage?

Each of these methods enables the student to go beyond simple factual recall and apply their learning in a flexible way.

Quiz to check understanding

True or false? *(Answers on p. 160)*

1. When you have enough surface learning, you naturally develop deep thinking.
2. Getting students to come up with their own hypotheses will only muddle them.
3. Use these methods only when your students have basic, surface knowledge secure.

FURTHER READING

Ceri Dean. (2012) *Classroom Instruction That Works.* Ch 9: Generating and testing hypotheses.

Institute for Educational Sciences. (2007) *Organizing Instruction and Study to Improve Student Learning.* Recommendation 7: Help students build explanations by asking and answering deep questions.

Geoff Petty. (2018) *Teach Even Better.* p 23: Surface learning and deep learning.

Feedback for improvement

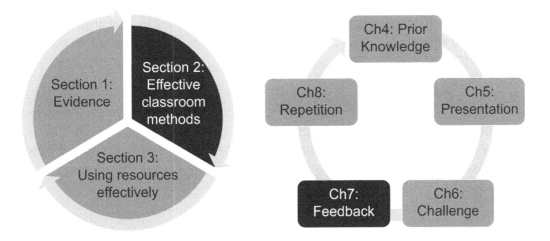

OVERVIEW

Feedback to the student is the process by which they get to know how well they are progressing, whether they are making mistakes (or have misconceptions) at this stage and guidance on how to improve/progress.

Feedback to the teacher is the knowledge of how well the students are learning. This lets you know whether you can safely move on or whether these students need a different approach, or more time.

There is therefore no one way to give feedback which is best. The vital point is that both you and your student act on the feedback.

Case study

Mr D is about to mark his Yr6 class assignment. He sets aside time at the weekend and writes careful feedback on each piece of work. On Monday morning, he hands out the work and instructs his students to read the feedback. He then spends much of the next hour going round his class explaining what his feedback means.

Mr D decides to do something different next time.

The method you choose needs to create a balance between the workload for you, the teacher, and the effect it will have on the learning of your student. Feedback is not the same as 'marking'; marking is just one way to give it.

The importance of feedback is illustrated by the fact that it is the only method which is a priority on each of the five main evidence sources we have used.

ABOUT FEEDBACK FOR IMPROVEMENT

There are different ways feedback can be given. It could be written, or verbal. It could be by the teacher, or by a peer, or they could get feedback themselves by marking their work from a mark scheme.

There are also different types of feedback given by teachers – and not all are helpful!

Quality of feedback

Not all feedback has the same effect. Hattie reports an experiment where the researchers sat at the back of classrooms and wrote down all the feedback they heard. Back in their lab the researchers then categorised the feedback into four types:

- Personal: This does not give any comment on the work, but is something like 'Well done' or 'You got grade C'.
- Task-based: The person giving the feedback gives the student the answer. Example: 'Put a full stop at the end of this sentence'.
- Process-based: The feedback is in the form of a question designed to tease out the answer. Example: 'What do you need at the end of a sentence?'
- Self-regulation: Some students already give themselves a self-feedback process. In the case of punctuation they self-check.

Self-regulation feedback aims to promote this type of self-regulation. Example: 'What strategy could you use to make sure your punctuation is correct?'

When the effectiveness of each method was assessed, they found that the first two types – personal and task-based – were largely ineffective. However, in the classes they observed, 80% of the feedback the students received was in those two categories.

Feedback is only effective when the student uses a thinking process to act on it.

To promote process-based feedback, as you go round the class, start to discipline yourself to give feedback only in the form of a question. This makes it much less likely you will either give the answer (task-based) or only making personal statements.

Of course, where you see good work or effort, feel free to offer praise. However, remember: praise is great; it's just that it isn't feedback!

Comments or marks?

Another piece of research compared the effect on learning of different types of feedback on a marked piece of work. Three groups of student who had completed the same task were either given:

- A mark
- Written feedback only
- Both a mark and feedback.

When the groups were re-assessed (to see the effect of the feedback) they found no improvement in the group given the mark, some improvement in the students given feedback, but, interestingly, no improvement in the students who received both feedback and a mark. It was as though the students were only interested in the mark/grade.

This suggests that, when giving written feedback, students should not get their mark at the same time. Return the work with comments only and only supply the mark once the improvement has been done.

However, students are used to getting their grade or mark and some do not like it when they receive only comments. Some students can be initially angry and want to know their score. You will need to tell them in advance about the new system and respond resolutely to their initial complaints.

Verbal feedback

There is an educational myth that the best form of feedback is written feedback. One reason for this is that, if the feedback is written in the book, then senior staff, inspectors and parents can see it. There is 'evidence'.

However, the research shows that the best feedback is that given while the task is in progress and the student can apply the feedback to improve the work. This means that looking over the student's shoulder as they work and making feedback comments is very effective.

You can also save time by combining verbal and written feedback.

Case study: Yr 9 Maths

Mr T is teaching Maths to an average Yr 9 class. All his written feedback in books to students is done in the lesson. He walks round with a pen in his hand. When he speaks to a student to help, he writes in the feedback so it is in their book and they can act on it. He comes back later to make sure the feedback has been acted on or if further help is needed.

ASSESSMENT AS FEEDBACK

Summative assessment

You have taught your students the topic and given them their assessment and marked their work. Sometimes called 'Assessment of learning', summative assessment simply gives you feedback on how well they have done, but it gives the student no opportunity to learn from the assessment process.

Formative assessment

Sometimes called 'Assessment for learning', this approach sometimes uses the same assessments, but marks them in a way which teaches the student something.

If you give the class a test and then mark it yourself and give them the mark, they will learn nothing from the process.

Self-assessment

One way to improve this process is self-assessment: they mark their own work, perhaps from a mark sheet or by you going through the questions with the whole class. This gives them feedback not only on what they got right, but also insight into what they got wrong. You may need to mark the work yourself if you need to record the summative mark as many teachers find that the higher-achieving students tend to under-mark their work while the lowest-achieving students over-mark.

However, if you don't need an accurate mark, there may be no need to worry. You can get a 'feel' for how much has been learned and the students have learned something during the marking process.

Peer assessment

Another route is peer assessment. This time each student marks another student's work. If they work in a pair then discussion along the lines of 'Why is that the right answer?' or 'Why didn't I get a mark there?'

This case study shows how one teacher realised he needed to approach the learning a different way.

Case study: Primary Maths

Mr B regularly sets his Yr 3 Maths class a short, ten-question quiz at the beginning of the lesson. He gives the students a mark to show them how well they have done. These quizzes cover the same skills, but with different numbers. However, he notices that marks are not improving. The mark does not tell the student how to improve and so is not effective feedback.

He changes tack. He still gives the same quiz, but he then groups students together who have made mistakes on a particular skill and works with them on the problem.

As understanding develops, test scores improve.

Another UK primary school uses a similar approach as school marking policy.

Case study: Yr 6 Maths

The Maths department now use 'Conferencing' to replace marking. At the end of the lesson the students mark their own work and highlight where they have met the 'success criteria'. Depending on the result, the students put their work into one of three trays: conferencing, non-conferencing or challenge.

Before the next Maths lesson the teacher reviews the 'Conferencing' tray and in the next lesson brings together all the students who had similar problems and, using pre-prepared material, guides their learning. Meanwhile the other students do an independent fluency task (itself a spaced repetition).

During the lesson the teacher has a stamp to mark the book where a mistake has been made or an improvement is needed. Students write in green pen to show that it is a response.

YELLOW BOX FEEDBACK

This is a technique to get over the problem that, if you have given written feedback on a large piece of work, not only is it hard to get the students to act on all of it, but it also takes ages!

The 'yellow box' technique is to use a highlighter pen to draw a box around the section you will comment on and then just give feedback on that. This way it is much easier to monitor that the student has made the improvement. It is also much easier for the student to know what needs improving without feeling overwhelmed.

QUESTIONING AS FEEDBACK

Feedback is a two-way process. As the teacher you need to know how well your students are doing and the student needs to know if they are on the right track with their learning.

Whole-class questioning can provide a quick way to check progress so long as you are aware of the limitations of some questioning methods.

Here are some common ways to question:

1. 'Hands-up' questioning. You ask a question and wait for hands up. You pick one student to answer. If their answer is correct, you give praise. If incorrect you try another hand.
2. Nominees answer (Cold Call). You ask the question in a similar way to 'hands up', but you choose who answers.
3. Pose, Pause, Pounce. Similar to Nominees answer, but you leave thinking time (pause) before you pounce on one student to answer.
4. Think, Pair, Share. You pose the question. Students first think on their own about the answer. They then discuss briefly with their partner (pair) before you invite them to share the answer with the class.
5. Buzz groups. Similar to Think, Pair Share, but the group is bigger than a pair – perhaps four students per 'buzz group'.
6. Assertive questioning. You pose the question and instruct the students to discuss the answer either in pairs or their buzz group. After some time you nominate one person to give the group reply. At this stage

you do not reveal the correct answer (if there is one!). You thank the student and ask another response. Then, if there is a difference of opinion you promote a class discussion and aim to develop a consensus. (Sometimes called 'Pose, Pause, Pounce, Bounce'.)

7. Mini-whiteboards (Show-me boards). Here the students are issued with small whiteboards and markers. They give their answer and then, at your signal, hold up the boards. You promote class discussion to reach a consensus.

But, which one to use? Groups of teachers have assessed each of these methods and judged them on four criteria:

- Level of participation by students.
- Feedback given to the student.
- The feedback you receive as a teacher about class progress.
- Whether you have given sufficient thinking time.

These teachers conclude that assertive questioning and mini-whiteboards score higher than the others. Using these criteria, 'Hands-up' questioning is judged the least effective because:

- Only a few students participate (usually the same ones!).
- Most other students did little thinking!
- Few students get feedback.
- You have little idea if the other students know the answer.

In some classrooms 'hands up' is still the most common questioning method. If you are choosing questioning to provide feedback to your students, then it's important to use an effective method.

WHY THIS METHOD WORKS

We know that learning consists of forming long-term memory links in the brain and that this is achieved by reusing these pathways (see Chapter 3).

Your students have seen/heard your presentation and are engaged in their challenging task. However, the student does not yet have secure knowledge. The task they are engaged with is part of the repetition process which will lead to long-term memories. If they make mistakes at this stage they will reinforce the incorrect links and learning will take much longer.

Feedback provides early intervention in the memory-forming process, aiming to ensure that the correct pathways are formed.

We need to remember that there is almost no way to remove a long-term memory from your student's brain once it is formed. This is why dealing with misconceptions is so hard. The correct answer will need to create an even stronger pathway than the wrong memory.

WHEN SHOULD I USE THIS METHOD IN MY CLASSROOM?

Feedback comes high on nearly every list of effective methods. You should choose a form of feedback which is most appropriate to your students and subject and apply it in a way which ensures that the student acts on the feedback.

PUTTING THIS METHOD INTO ACTION

Assertive questioning: 'Pose, pause, pounce, bounce'

If you haven't used this type of questioning before with your class, you will need to brief them beforehand that, if you 'bounce' the question to another group before giving the correct answer, this does not mean that their answer was wrong.

- Pick a question.
- Say something like: 'I'm going to ask you a question. Discuss this with your neighbour for about 30 seconds and then I'm going to pick someone to answer. If I pick you, you should report your discussion, not your personal opinion'.
- Pose the question.
- Pause for discussion (it often doesn't take long).
- Pounce on a student. (In the early stages you can pounce on someone who you notice has not been discussing the question. You will find that, after some practice, the class gets used to this method and almost all students participate.)
- Listen to their answer and then ask how or why they arrived at it.
- Bounce the question to another person. Again listen and ask how/ why?

After about three bounces you will detect three main types of response:

1. All correct answers. Ask if any group have a different answer. Clear up any misconceptions.

2. Several different answers, some right, some wrong. Start a class discussion. 'Jane, your group thought A, because..., but Bill your group thought B, because... Sunjay, does your group agree with either?' After a bit of this 'assertive questioning' you may gradually detect a consensus emerging. If this consensus is correct it gives you great feedback that the class now substantially understand the idea.

3. If no consensus emerges, or if the consensus is wrong, this gives great feedback that the concept is not understood. You now know that your original teaching was not good enough. You will need to use the Learning Cycle to work out where the fault occurred and plan to reteach.

Quiz to check understanding

True or false? *(Answers on p. 161)*

1. It doesn't matter if students are not shown their errors soon enough, they can be easily corrected.
2. Feedback is not effective if students do not act on it.
3. Students need to be given enough thinking time when a question is posed.
4. Praise can be counterproductive.

FURTHER READING

FEEDBACK

Allison and Tharby. (2015) *Making Every Lesson Count*. Ch 5: Feedback.
Ceri Dean. (2012) *Classroom Instruction that Works*. Ch1: Providing feedback.
Education Endowment Foundation. *Toolkit*. Online resource: Feedback.
Dylan Wiliam. (2011) *Embedded formative assessment*. Ch 5: Providing feedback that moves learning forward.

QUESTIONING

Allison and Tharby. (2015) *Making Every Lesson Count*. Ch 6: Questioning.
Institute for Educational Sciences. (2007) *Organizing Instruction and Study to Improve Student Learning*. Recommendation 5b: Use quizzes to re-expose students to information.

8

Repetition and consolidation

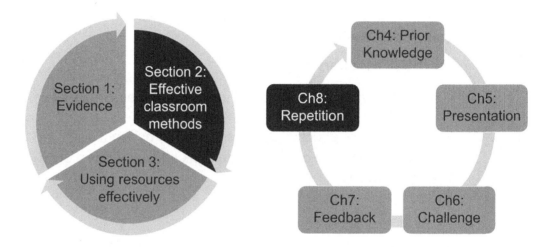

OVERVIEW

Most short-term memories formed in the lesson will fade within a few days unless reinforced. Some form of spaced repetition is vital to form long-term memories. Your students need to exercise the same pathway at least three times after the initial teaching to achieve this.

Case study

Ms B has been teaching her class about the rivers in South America. They have sketched the rivers onto a continent outline and stuck it in their books. The following week she gives them a starter activity – a similar outline map and a list of the rivers. Most students do not start. She asks what the problem is. 'We haven't done this, Miss'. is the reply. Ms B assures them they did it last week. Student Becky is insistent that they have not. 'Just turn back in your exercise book'. Ms B assures her. Becky turns back two pages and sees the map. 'Did I do that?' she exclaims.

Both Ms B and Becky are shocked that the memory seems to have disappeared.

However good your presentation, however enthusiastic your teaching, however good your marking, unless your students use the same memory-pathway several times over the days/weeks ahead, the memory will fade.

ABOUT REPETITION AND CONSOLIDATION

There are numerous ways to give students the opportunity to practice:

- Quick-fire quiz
- Written test
- Homework (a practice, not an extension task)
- Assertive questioning
- Peer explaining
- Card sorting.

It is less important which method you use than that the students get those repetition opportunities. However, experiments show that retrieval practice is more effective than simply seeing/hearing the information again (e.g. re-reading).

There are, however, a few things to consider in making your choice.

Spaced v massed practice

Let's compare these two approaches. Figure 8.1 illustrates the difference. The light grey boxes represent the lessons where new material is presented and applied for the first time. The dark grey boxes are lessons of revision. In 'massed practice', all the practice takes place at the end of the topic. In 'spaced practice', it is spread out.

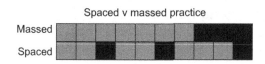

FIGURE 8.1

The new topic will be covered in ten lessons. There are seven parts to the topic and the topic test is taken at the end. Mr R takes one class, Ms S the other.

Mr R uses massed practice: In lesson one he covers Part 1, the students do the activity for Part 1 and many appear to have learned. They may even be set homework on Part 1.

In lesson two, Mr R moves on to Part 2 and activity 2. The topic continues until all the material is covered. All seems well. After covering the seven parts, Mr R gives the class time to revise the whole topic before the test.

At first, this looks like a reasonable approach; indeed, it is a very common one. However, this approach has been shown in experiments to be significantly less effective than the following.

Ms S uses spaced practice: In her class, in the first lesson, Ms S follows the same pattern as Mr R, but, at the start of lesson 2, she gives the class a quick-fire quiz on what they covered in lesson 1. She has the students mark their own work, does not collect the marks, but has a quick show of hands for higher marks to see how many students have good recall of lesson 1.

She then covers the material more quickly than Mr R, does activity 2 and still finds time for five min assertive questioning covering material from both lessons.

At the end of lesson 3 Ms S sets homework covering material from all three lessons. She does not use lesson 6 to introduce new material, but to consolidate the first five lessons. She progresses like this, presenting new material giving activates, etc., but interspersed with regular short quizzes, homework and plenary questioning interludes.

Her students take the same test as Mr R's class. Their results are significantly better.

WHY THIS METHOD WORKS

As we saw in Chapter 3, for long-term memories to be formed, a specific change needs take place at the junctions of the brain cells (the synapses of the neurons) called *long-term potentiation*. This can only happen if the same pathway is activated on several different occasions before the synapse reverts to its original state.

This means that spaced repetition is an absolute necessity.

Some students may appear to learn without the specific repetitions you plan for the whole class. This is not because their brains are working differently, it is because they do the repetitions themselves by mulling the material over or doing the repetitions outside the classroom.

Case study
Ms T is explaining to her Yr 11 class about the need for spaced repetitions to secure long-term memories. A girl asks a question about her friend: 'What about Belinda? She does almost no work in the class and still gets an "A"'.

Ms T is curious and asks Belinda if she revises outside the topic. Belinda is reluctant to answer. 'Yyeess' she says, hesitantly, not wanting to appear as a 'swot' in front of her friends. Ms T asks what she does. 'I read the textbook', she confesses. Her friends are amazed. 'You read the TEXTBOOK?! When do you do that?!' Belinda explains she does it at home. Her parents have bought copies of the textbooks she uses at school. She says she reads them 'When I'm bored'.

Her friends quiz her on how many times she had read the textbook for this class. Again Belinda is reluctant to reveal her work. 'Only three or four times…', she admits.

Ms T says nothing. Belinda has made the point perfectly.

Belinda has used re-reading as a repetition method in this example. It has worked for her, but is not the best method.

Some writers argue that a certain amount of forgetting needs to take place before any repetition for it to be effective. A simpler explanation is that the repetitions need to be spaced and that during that space a certain amount of forgetting takes place. The evidence seems to point for the need for repetitions to be spaced in time. The 'forgetting' is secondary.

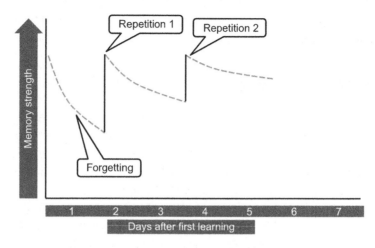

FIGURE 8.2

Spacing of practice

There is no hard-and-fast rule about the spacing which is most effective, but the repeats do need to occur before the learning is completely forgotten.

Figure 8.2 shows the formation of long-term memories. The initial rate of forgetting is high. We know this because we so often see this in the classroom.

In Ms B's class the students did not get the first repetition before the memory had completely faded. The teacher in this case study does better.

Case study: Secondary English
Mr K knows that repetition is important, so he revisits key ideas like 'alliteration', 'metaphor' and 'onomatopoeia' several times. He is sure the class will know what these are, and so he tests his class. About 80% of the students get top marks and are quite shocked at the 20% who still do not know what these words mean.

Mr K then realises that the 20% are the students who have not offered an answer when he does his questioning: 'Spot the onomatopoeia in this sentence'. They don't know it because, for them, repetition did not happen.

He switches tack and uses a 'no-hands-up' questioning technique which makes sure every student tries to answer the question.

Case study: Yr 4 English

Mr E's school have adopted a template for a whole-class reading session. On the Monday he introduces the new text and pulls out about four tricky words. Students then have to define the word, give examples in a sentence and find antonyms and synonyms. These words are revisited at the start of each reading session. Students have to use the words in different contexts.

Interweaved practice

Interweaved practice involves revising material from earlier topics interweaved with material from the current topic. It is effective because it is a practical way to do spaced repetition. Without interweaved practice, once a topic is finished, there is no opportunity to revisit it and secure long-term memories (LTMs).

One suggestion is that, when setting the quiz, pick questions not only from the last lesson, but from last week, last topic and last term as well.

Case study: Yr 2 Maths

Every Friday Mr R gives his students a fluency-based activity where they revisit all the learning for the past week and also other previous learning. This week they were doing subtraction, but the Friday session includes questions on place-value, on addition and on money which they covered earlier. Any misconceptions can be picked up and dealt with while the other students are practicing.

WHEN SHOULD I USE THIS METHOD IN MY CLASSROOM?

Spaced repetition is vital. You should use it with every topic.

This is one technique which does not require practice before you try it. Clearly, as you use spaced and interweaved practice more you will become more skilled in their use, but, since the LTMs we want in our students can only be built with spaced repetitions, any opportunities you can create will be beneficial. Assuming your students have understood the material, it's difficult to see how repetition can 'go wrong'.

PUTTING THIS METHOD INTO ACTION

1. Look at the current plan you have for teaching the topic.
2. Identify the current revision opportunities: quiz, homework, etc.

3. Assess whether you have given your students the opportunity to revisit/retrieve the material at least three times (not including the first lesson).
4. If not, re-arrange or add opportunities to your plan.

You will need to make space for this by spending less time on some things you would normally do, but the evidence suggests that, overall, the learning will improve.

Quiz to check understanding

True or false? *(Answers on p. 161)*

1. So long as repetitions take place, the timing is unimportant.
2. New learning practice must always be interweaved with other subject learning.
3. Without repetition, new memories can be quickly and completely forgotten.

FURTHER READING

Allison and Tharby. (2015) *Making Every Lesson Count*. Ch 4: Practice.
Ceri Dean. (2012) *Classroom Instruction That Works*. Ch 7: Assigning homework and Providing practice.
Institute for Educational Sciences. (2007) *Organizing Instruction and Study to Improve Student Learning*. Recommendation 1: Space learning over time. Recommendation 2: Interleave worked example solutions and problem-solving exercises.
Barak Rosenshine. (2012) *Principles of Instruction*. Principle 9: Independent practice.

3

USING RESOURCES EFFECTIVELY

INTRODUCTION

Chapter 9: *'Using resources effectively'* looks at five areas where care should be taken to ensure the best use of human and financial resources in things outside the classroom:

Reducing workload: identifies time-consuming, but ineffective methods and the value of refocussing on the best time-value methods.

Staff development: explains how much CPD time/money is often wasted due to insufficient follow-up. It shows the need for teachers to practice with a limited number of methods over an extended period and the importance of allocating time for this to happen.

Teaching Assistants: introduces the research that shows that, while some uses of Teaching Assistants have been shown to be ineffective, other uses are highly effective.

Technology: shows that simply having the technology is ineffective. Technology works best when it improves the implementation of proven methods.

Avoiding myths and low-effect methods: Shows that the easiest way to save on resources is to simply stop doing things which are ineffective.

9

Using resources effectively

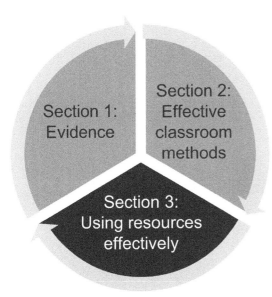

Ch9: Using resources effectively

This chapter covers five areas of school/college resources and discusses ways to use those human and/or financial resources most effectively:

- Teacher workload
- Staff development
- Teaching Assistants
- Information technology
- Myths and low-effect methods.

TEACHER WORKLOAD

Although this is probably not a conscious decision, some managers act as though the more they give teachers to do, the more their students will learn.

However, this is clearly not the case. If the front-line workers (the teachers) become overworked, not only does their work suffer, but they are more likely to take sick leave and even to leave the profession. Figure 9.1 shows the pattern. Initially, the more hours a teacher works, the more learning the students make. However, it reaches a peak and learning goes into decline as teachers become more tired, stressed, ill, etc.

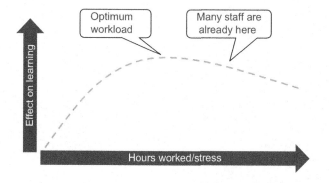

FIGURE 9.1

Reducing workload

When senior staff give teachers additional tasks they often do so based only on the value of the new task. They may, for instance, require marking of students' work to be more regular, or in a different format. They may show evidence that this new method is effective – and that could be true. However, if a teacher has to make time for a new task, they will have less time for other tasks. The task they now omit may have a greater effect on learning than the imposed new task – so, the overall level of learning declines.

The first rule for reducing workload is to ensure this does not happen.

Some admin tasks can be time-consuming. For instance, a judgement needs to be made on how many summative tests are necessary to assess student progress during the course. Sometimes, where the accurate mark is not needed, use of peer or self-assessment or the use of voting pads can considerably reduce teacher workload.

A great way to identify tasks which can be scrapped or reduced is to consult the teachers. An anonymous survey can quickly reveal tasks which most teachers think are unnecessary. Of course, they may not always be right; in general, however, the teachers want the best for their pupils and are aware of the need to prioritise.

STAFF DEVELOPMENT

The importance of staff development is illustrated by Figure 9.2.

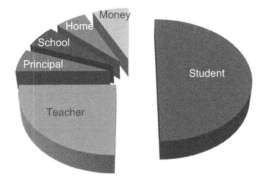

FIGURE 9.2

The whole circle represents all the influences on the student at the time they take their exam at the end of your course. Approximately 50% is due to the student themselves – it is the combination of their genetics, family background, life chances, etc. prior to your teaching.

However, of the remaining 50%, half is down to the teacher. All the other influences are relatively unimportant.

This means that the best way to improve the learning of the students in a school/college is to develop the skills of the teacher. More money, a new principal/headteacher, different school type, etc. are much less important.

An illustration of the importance of the teacher can be seen if we compare the effect of the school as a whole with the effect of the individual teacher. If two similar students attend two colleges, one rated 'outstanding' and the other 'needing improvement', the difference in outcome between the two students (if we look at statistical averages) is small. However, if those same two students attend the same college but have different teachers, the effect on their learning can be a factor of two.

If the average progress of the average student with the average teacher in one year in 100, then, with a weak teacher, the learning could easily be 75, while a strong teacher could help the student make progress of 150, making a good teacher twice as effective as one with weak teaching skills.

However, 'plasticity', the science which explains that we should be more optimistic about the possibility of our students to improve their learning, also applies to teachers. All teachers can improve their teaching skills so long as they are taken (or take themselves) through the Learning Cycle.

The most cost-effective way to improve the overall school/college results is to improve the skills of the weakest teachers. However, to do so would be divisive as those teachers would be labelled while other teachers would not make progress. In practice, the best approach is to develop the skills of the whole staff.

Effective staff development

Every 10 years or so, a research team receive funding to review the evidence about the effectiveness of staff training in schools. Interestingly, they all come to a similar conclusion in one area, illustrated by this case study.

Case study

Ms W is an able and effective head of department and good teacher. On a Friday before half-term, she attends a training day in her own subject. Returning to school a week later, she enthuses to her colleague about how great the training session was and how she will raise some of the ideas in the next department meeting. Ms G asks Ms W for an example of these great ideas. Ms W thinks for a minute and then says she cannot recall anything in detail, but will check her notes.

Ms W never raises the subject again and there nothing from the training day appears on the next department meeting agenda. When Ms G raises the issue, Ms W apologises and says there were other, more urgent matters.

Now that we know about the Learning Cycle, we can see why this happened. Ms W attended sessions which introduced new ideas. At the time these were delivered, Ms W could link the new learning to her Prior Knowledge and judge the ideas to be ones she wanted to try and share in the department. However, there was no opportunity for her to consolidate the memories as there was no challenging task, feedback or repetition to secure long-term memories.

Like all short-term memories, even by Monday they had started to fade. By the time she was writing the agenda for the next department meeting, the detail in these short-term memories had almost completely faded and the only thing she could remember was the positive emotion she had experienced.

What the research shows is that what happened to Ms W happens to the vast majority of teachers. If you:

- Attend a training session (external or in-house).
- Hear about some new ideas.
- Discuss how you might use them in your teaching.
- Try out the idea in the training session.

If you then either do not try it out in your own teaching, or, if you do try it, you quickly give up as it didn't go well, then the research shows what you'd expect it to show – that the time and money spent on that INSET was mostly wasted.

Fortunately, the research also shows what *does* work.

- Senior staff at your school/college make a strategic decision to go evidence-based.
- The whole staff, including managers, attend training sessions which introduce evidence-based teaching methods.
- Staff meet regularly in groups of three or four to support each other. These groups should be autonomous, in the sense that they decide for themselves what they are going to do. (These groups are known by a number of different names: Supported Experiments, Action Research, Peer Mentoring, and Professional Learning Communities.)
- You identify your learning needs and pick one or two methods which address these needs. You try these out in the classroom – with the knowledge that it might not go well the first time.
- In your small group, you discuss how it went and how to improve.
- You try the method again several times, and get feedback by self-assessment and peer observation, or through discussion and reflection (no senior staff are present at this stage).
- After about three attempts, you will know if this method will work for you, your subject, and your students.
- After about 10 tries, you will become competent.

■ After about 25 repeated uses over a period of 6–24 months, the method will become integrated into your teaching 'schema' and the use of the method will become one you turn to naturally in your normal planning. You will then start to achieve the effect-sizes shown by the research.

Providing time for professional development

The research also shows that, unless teachers are given time to develop their skills and their CPD is organised in such a way that each teacher has to show what they have been working on, then, due to all the other pressures and priorities, effective methods will not be practiced and learning will not improve.

In this case study we see a real example of how spending less time teaching actually leads to better student learning.

Case study

The senior team at a UK secondary school realise the value of action research, but they also realise that staff do not have time to engage with it. They take the dramatic decision to close the school early on Fridays. Students leave after lunch.

With every Friday afternoon available for their research, all teachers benefit. The school is judged 'outstanding'.

TEACHER AS RESEARCHER?

Looking back at the evidence section in Part 1 we can see that, for evidence from classroom experiments to be valid (i.e., reliable and useful to others), we need large numbers of students, several different classes, control groups and independent assessment. There is no way that a single classroom teacher can create these conditions.

Some models of 'action research' encourage teachers to try something for themselves in their own classroom, evaluate it themselves and perhaps compare their results with another class or a previous year's results. This is not a totally pointless exercise because any process which focusses the teacher on whether the students are learning is likely to have a positive effect. However, we need to be clear that this type of research does not create evidence of sufficient quality for others to follow.

Furthermore, when given a free choice, teachers can easily experiment with a method which has already been shown to be relatively ineffective. For instance, 'Gender Differences' is one of the most popular subjects – but the overwhelming evidence from hundreds of experiments is that teaching males and females in different ways is not effective.

Teachers can make an effective contribution to original research by participating in well-organised research by outside organisations such as the Education Endowment Foundation (EEF). Your class could act as either a control or an intervention group.

However, the most effective model for teachers is the one described above where you 'experiment with' a method which already has good evidence of effectiveness. Your experiment is to find out how to get this method to work with you, your students and your subject.

With so many effective methods to choose from and with the need to practice each one over an extended period, most of us will not need to get to the point of trying something untested.

TEACHING ASSISTANTS (TAs)

The effective deployment of Teaching Assistants is a complex affair which this book does not aim to cover in detail. What follows is a summary of the findings of a major report generated by EEF published as *Making best use of Teaching Assistants*.

Since 2000, there has been a tripling in the number of TAs in UK schools. However, the 'Deployment and Impact of Support Staff (DISS)' project showed that much of the effect of TAs on the learning of the targeted students was negative.

One suggested reason is that too much support can create dependency by removing the ownership and responsibility for learning. Another is that TAs are often focussed on task completion – getting their student to actually finish the task, rather than on developing their understanding.

One way to see this is to look back to the research on feedback. Table 9.1 illustrates the different types of verbal feedback.

Table 9.1

Feedback type	Example
Personal	'Well done'; 'You got grade C'
Task-based	'Put a full stop at the end of this sentence'.
Process-based	'What do you need at the end of a sentence?'
Self-regulation	'What strategy could you use to make sure your punctuation is correct?'

One reason TAs can be ineffective is that they give far too much of their feedback as types 1 and 2 (Personal and Task-based), neither of which leads to additional learning.

On the other hand, classroom teachers support having a TA in the classroom as they can help with routine tasks and discipline, allowing the teacher more time to teach. This means, ironically, that the main beneficiaries of the TA are not to target students – but the teacher and the other pupils!

The same EEF report combined evidence from various sources to give seven components of effective use of TAs:

1. Low-attaining students should be taught by the teacher, not by the TA.
2. Use TAs to add value to what the teacher does, not replace them.
3. Use TAs to help pupils develop independent learning skills and manage their own learning.
4. Ensure TAs are sufficiently familiar with the material in the lesson that they will be able to help students' understanding.
5. Use TAs to deliver high-quality one-to-one support using structured interventions.
6. Adopt only evidence-based interventions. (Most have no evidence to support their use.)

TECHNOLOGY

There is no evidence that simply having the technology is effective. Technology works best when it improves the implementation of proven methods.

Technology seemed to offer so much to teaching. Our students would enthusiastically sit in front of screen attending to the tasks we had set them, learning at their own pace and getting feedback from the software.

Unfortunately, research on the effectiveness of teaching technology shows very mixed results. Simply using the technology seems to have almost no effect on learning.

Many teachers have had experiences like these:

■ Setting homework which uses the Internet, only to hear lame excuses about some problem with their home technology.
■ Planning a great lesson on the IT suite, but have to spend half our time policing the room.
■ Bringing in the set of laptops and spent too much time with faulty machines, flat batteries, mindless vandalism, etc.

Therefore, before using a technology solution, ask one key question: Is using this technology better than the non-tech approach? Unless the clear answer is 'Yes', then, use technology with caution.

However, if we look at the Learning Cycle we can see how technology could be applied at each step.

1   Prior Knowledge: Use voting pads or online quizzes to assess your students.
2   Presenting new material: Use video, animation or slides to provide 'dual coding'. Use mapping software to create your Advance Organiser and extend it during the course.
3   Setting challenging tasks: Students use graphical software to create Graphical Organisers. Use a presenter to project group work to the whole class for discussion.
4   Feedback and improvement: Use online assessments and voting pads to provide feedback to students on their progress.
5   Repetition: Use calendar software to set repetitions for your class to help remind you of the spaced or interweaved repetition. Send social media messages with homework tasks or one-question quizzes.

Some general guidelines for the effective use of technology:

- To implement an evidence-based method, for example, mind-mapping software, or displaying graphics or animations.
- Employ a teacher who has been trained both in the technical side and the pedagogical (learning) value of the technology.
- For short, focused sessions, rather than for the whole course.
- In catch-up sessions for lower-achieving or disadvantaged students.
- To free the teacher up to spend more time helping students.
- In ways that helps the students to work harder at the task.
- To work collaboratively in small groups or pairs of students.

MYTHS AND LOW-EFFECT METHODS

The easiest way to save on resources is simply to stop doing things which are either myths or have been shown to be ineffective. This is a quick run-through of some common ideas which have been proposed but which are not worth the time/effort/cost.

Your students are not 'left-brained or 'right-brained', nor are there significant gender differences in the learning of males and females. They do not have learning styles or learning preferences. The most common of these is Visual, Auditory and Kinaesthetic (VAK). Research to test this has always proved negative.

There are no 'superfoods' which enhance learning, a balanced diet is best for the brain. Students do not need water available all the time (e.g., water bottle on the desk). If water is available at break times, that is sufficient.

There is no evidence to support the playing of Mozart or other music to promote learning.

It is not better to be taught by a teacher who is expert in their subject knowledge (well above that needed to teach the course), nor is it necessarily helpful for teachers to be given longer teacher training.

The average results of students taught in mixed-ability groups are not significantly different from those taught in sets or ability groups. Lower-achieving students benefit from mixed-ability while the highest-achieving students do better in the top set.

Changes to the school day, whether in the starting time or the length of the lesson, have no significant effect.

Increased school finances are not well correlated with outcomes. Paying teachers or students on results has not proved effective. New buildings have no significant effect unless the previous buildings were unsuitable, derelict, etc.

Being an academy, a charter school or a free school does not automatically lead to higher standards. It's the schools who implement effective methods who do better.

Reducing class sizes (say from 30 to 25) has little effect and is not cost-effective. Learning does not rise significantly until the class is down to about 12 or less.

EFFECTIVE USE OF RESOURCES: SUMMARY

- Overloading teachers with new tasks does not improve students' learning.
- Improving teachers' skills is the best way to improve students' results.
- Teachers need time to implement their Action Research.
- Teaching Assistants (TAs), used incorrectly, can inhibit the learning of the student they are helping. However, trained TAs implementing small-group interventions are highly effective.

- Technology should only be used to implement evidence-based methods and then only if it is an advantage over non-tech solutions.
- If a new method or policy is suggested, check for evidence of effectiveness first. Do not rely on a persuasive argument.

... AND FINALLY

The teaching profession is not yet evidence-based. You will continue to be bombarded with policies and methods, all claiming to be effective, by senior leaders, parents, book authors, bloggers, journalists and politicians.

Arm yourself with the evidence and ask them for theirs.

Appendix A:
Sources of evidence

FIVE MAIN SOURCES (RESEARCH REVIEWS)

Ceri Dean. (2012) *Classroom Instruction that Works*. ASCD.
Education Endowment Foundation. *Toolkit*. Online resource.
John Hattie. (2012) *Visible Learning for Teachers*. Routledge.
Institute for Educational Sciences. (2007) *Organizing Instruction and Study to Improve Student Learning*.
Barak Rosenshine. (2012) *Principles of Instruction*. International Academy of Education.

SUPPLEMENTARY SOURCES

Allison and Tharby. (2015) *Making Every Lesson Count*. Crown House
Brown, Roediger and McDaniel. (2014) *Make it Stick*.
Chartered College of Teaching. (2020) Impact No. 8: Cognition and learning.
Churches et al. (2017) *Neuroscience for Teachers*. Crown House.
Deans for Impact. (2015). *The Science of Learning*. Austin, TX: Deans for Impact.
Fletcher-Wood et al. (2018) *The Learning Curriculum*. Institute for Teaching (IfT).
Geoff Petty. (2018) *Teach Even Better*. Oxford University Press.
Sherrington and Caviglioli. (2020) *Teaching WalkThrus*. John Catt.

Top 20 Principles from Psychology for PreK–12 Teaching and Learning. Coalition for Psychology in Schools and Education (CPSE), 2015.

Dylan Wiliam (2011) *Embedded Formative Assessment.* Solution Tree.

LINKS TO ONLINE RESOURCES

Direct links to online resources listed above can be found on this page: http://ebtn.org.uk/links-and-resources/.

Appendix B
Answers to quizzes in Section 2

PRIOR KNOWLEDGE QUIZZES

Explanations for many of these questions can be found in Chapter 3.

Chapter 4

Quit

1. Long-term memories are formed by repetitions.
   True. One visit is not sufficient.

2. Long-Term Memory and Working Memory work in similar ways.
   False. Working memories last a few seconds and do not permanently change the brain.

3. Memories in the brain are similar to memories on a computer.
   False. Computers store all the data and can 'remember' perfectly. Brains create links to prior knowledge.

Chapter 5

Method 1: Working Memory limit

1. Most students can store around seven items in their Working Memory.
   True. When tested, this is the average number of items that can be recalled.

2. Working Memory capacity changes with age, with the peak reached in mid-teens.
   True. Younger children have less working memory.

3. All students of the same age have the same Working Memory capacity.
   False. Working Memory capacity is closely linked to IQ.

4. Having good Long-Term Memories frees up Working Memory space.
   True.

Method 2: Linking to Prior Knowledge

1. Prior Knowledge is important, but not vital to learning.
   False. It is vital. The students cannot think about something they do not have memories to connect to.

2. Prior Knowledge is what the student has learned in previous lessons on this topic.
   False. It includes this, but also includes all the memories in the schema.

3. New long-term memories can be formed instantly.
   False. All memories need spaced repetition to secure them.

Method 3: Multi-sensory approach

1. Students use several senses at a time to access learning.
   True. Sight, sound, touch and emotion all play a part.

2. Students have individual 'learning styles' which favour one sense.
   False. Experiments show students do not learn more quickly when taught in the 'preferred style'.

3. Some students are weak in processing information from one sense (e.g. hearing).
   True. A multi-sensory approach benefits all students.

Chapter 6

Method 2: Graphical and non-linguistic methods

1. Long-term memories are stored in the brain as connections between neurons.
    True.

2. 'Dual coding' involves explaining the new concept in two different ways.
    False. Dual coding means using two different senses, usually words and images.

3. When you first try a new method in the classroom it may not work well.
    True. You need long-term memories of using the method.

Method 5: Thinking tasks

1. New knowledge is connected to prior knowledge.
    True.

2. If you are well prepared, when you first try a new method in the classroom it will go well.
    False. You may be brilliant or lucky, but usually a new method takes several attempts to master.

3. Memories are links to the components of the memory.
    True. What we call a new memories is simply the links to its components.

Chapter 8

Repetition and consolidation

1. Long-term memories are formed once the student has understood the new idea.
    False. Students can easily completely forget something they understood in your lesson.

2. The brain has almost limitless capacity for learning as new knowledge links to prior knowledge.
    True. There is no evidence of the brain 'filling up'.

3. When long-term memories are formed, a physical change takes place at the synapse which can last a lifetime.
True. Long-term memory is a physical change.

QUIZZES TO CHECK UNDERSTANDING

Chapter 4

Prior Knowledge

1. New learning does not need to be linked to prior knowledge.
False.

2. Missing Prior Knowledge is a serious impediment to learning.
True. It is better to spend time filling in missing knowledge, rather than focussing only on the new material.

3. Vocabulary is Prior Knowledge for all learning, so vocabulary checks and repair are vital.
True.

4. Phonics is Prior Knowledge for reading.
Generally true. Weak phonics is often a component in poor reading skills.

5. You do not have time to repair Prior Knowledge.
False. You will save time in the long run as the learning will be quicker.

Chapter 5

Method 1: Working Memory limit

1. Having a decorated area around the board helps students learn.
False. It can create distraction and use Working Memory.

2. All students have the same amount of Working Memory.
False. Working Memory is linked to age and intelligence.

3. Rote learning frees up space in working memory.
True. But only if the learning has already been understood.

Method 2: Link to Prior Knowledge

1. Linking to Prior Knowledge is linking to what you taught them in the previous lesson.
    False. Prior Knowledge includes all the knowledge the student needs to link in the new learning.

2. Linking to Prior Knowledge makes physical links in the brain of your student to memories they already have.
    True.

3. Students will make their own links; you don't need to show them the links.
    False. Some students may see the links, but do not rely on this.

Method 3: Multi-sensory approach

1. Students have different 'learning styles'. You need to use the different senses to allow all students to learn.
    False. Students do not have learning styles. You use different senses to make better memories and allow for weaknesses.

2. You create stronger memories if it contains more than one sensory component.
    True.

3. We all have both visual and auditory Working Memory, so it makes sense to make use of both types.
    True.

Method 4: Advance Organisers

1. Students store knowledge in two levels – the detail and the big picture. An Advance Organiser gives students the big picture first.
    True.

2. You should not use Advance Organisers with good readers as it inhibits their learning.
    False. Some students benefit less from your Advance Organiser, but it is not a hindrance.

3. It is important to create your Advance Organiser exactly as described here, otherwise it will not be effective.
    False. The important point is to communicate the 'big picture'. Any method that succeeds is valid.

Method 5: Linking abstract ideas to concrete analogies

1. Quiz programs like *Mastermind* test abstract thinking.
    False. They are factual recall.

2. Abstract Ideas cannot be directly experiences with the senses.
    True. They need concrete analogies.

3. Linking an Abstract Idea to a concrete example is helpful, but not vital.
    False. All new learning needs to be linked to Prior Knowledge.

Chapter 6

Method 1: Modelling and Worked Examples

1. Most students can understand the task if it is explained well.
    False. Some can, but do not assume this will happen.

2. Worked Examples show what the final product should be like.
    False. Not just the final product, but also the process to create it.

3. The best Worked Examples are generated by the teacher.
    False. The method works so long as the student knows what the product will be like and how to get there. Any process which achieves this is effective.

Method 2: Graphical and non-linguistic methods

1. A 'challenging task' is one which the students find difficult.
    False. The task needs to be achievable with a struggle, but not so difficult that the student fails to achieve it.

2. Using multi-sensory methods confuses the student and makes learning slower.
    False. Multiple senses make better memories (so long as Working Memory is not overloaded).

3. So long as you are well planned, it is safe to try out a new teaching method for a whole lesson.
    Usually false. It is safer to try something for just a few minutes first time.

Method 3: Metacognition

1. Metacognition is only relevant for older students.
    False. 'How did you do that?' and 'What if...?' questions can be used in primary school.

2. Students with good metacognitive skills achieve higher grades.
    True.

3. Metacognitive skills developed in one subject can be used in other subjects and situations.
    True.

Method 4: Collaborative methods

1. Working in groups does not work as some students will do nothing towards the task.
    False. This is only true if you do not assign roles/tasks to individuals.

2. Collaborative work improves learning by using dialogue to promote thinking.
    True.

3. Collaborative tasks work best when you are introducing new material.
    False. It works best to consolidate knowledge.

Method 5: Thinking tasks

1. When you have enough surface learning, you naturally develop deep thinking.
    False. Most students need a thinking task to connect their factual knowledge and make it usable in other situations.

2. Getting students to come up with their own hypotheses will only muddle them.
    False. The aim is for them to test their hypothesis.

3. Use these methods only when your students have basic, surface knowledge secure.
    True. It is not successful if used too early in the topic.

Chapter 7

Feedback for improvement

1. It doesn't matter if students are not shown their errors soon enough, they can be easily corrected.
    False. It is much harder to change a long-term memory than to correct it while it is being formed.

2. Feedback is not effective if students do not act on it.
    True. That is why the chapter is called 'Feedback for Improvement' and not just 'Feedback'.

3. Students need to be given enough thinking time when a question is posed.
    True.

4. Praise can be counterproductive.
    True. Praise alone can be good for self-esteem, etc., but it is not feedback as the student does not know how to improve.

Chapter 8

Repetition and consolidation

1. So long as repetitions take place, the timing is unimportant.
    False. Repetitions too soon or too late may have no effect.

2. New learning practice must always be interweaved with other subject learning.
    False. This is good practice, but not necessary. It is the spaced repletion which works, interweaving is one method.

3. Without repetition, new memories can be quickly and completely forgotten.
    True. The synapse can 'reset' to the same state it was before the learning and so register no memory at all.

Index

Made in the USA
Monee, IL
06 August 2021